Ebbets to Paradise-O'Malley's Journey to the Coliseum & Dodger Stadium
Allen Schery

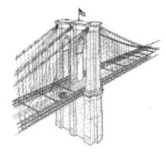

Brooklyn Bridge Books

Brooklyn Bridge Books

Copyright © [Year of First Publication] by [Author or Pen Name]

All rights reserved.

No portion of this book may be reproduced in any form without written permission from the publisher or author, except as permitted by U.S. copyright law.

ISBN

This work is dedicated to childhood idol and later life friend "Duke" Snider. In the 1980's, as Allen attended multiple Sports Collector conventions to build up his Dodger Collection, he and Duke constantly ran into one another. Allen had a 1950's Don Newcombe warm-up jacket and several Dodger player jerseys in an era where none were available. Duke jokingly asked Allen if he had an inside deal with their equipment manager, Allen for his part jokingly asked Duke if he was stalking him! Today Allen lives 20 miles North of Fallbrook where Duke had his Avocado Ranch and Bowling Alley and has visited his old friend's gravesite wearing one of Duke's number four jerseys. As you can see below no one would even know this was a former famous baseball players gravesite.

Art

Sports artist LeRoy Neiman was commissioned to celebrate the 100th Anniversary of the Dodger organization in 1990, which included Dodger Stadium and Ebbets Field, as well as (from the top) Fernando Valenzuela, Jackie Robinson, Kirk Gibson, Zack Wheat, Duke Snider, and Sandy Koufax.

About the Author

Allen Schery's lifelong passion for the Dodgers began in infancy, growing up near Ebbets Field in Brooklyn where the voices of Vin Scully and Red Barber filled his childhood. Living near the Ebbets Field site, he was immersed in the team's culture from his earliest days. Beginning his collection of Dodger memorabilia at age five, Schery has amassed what is widely regarded as the world's largest private Dodgers collection, with over 250,000 artifacts ranging from player pins and pennants to rare photographs, bobbleheads, and historic documents and anything Dodger. His deep personal connection to the team includes friendships with legendary players such as Pee Wee Reese, Gil Hodges, Roy Campanella, Duke Snider, Don Newcombe, and Jackie Robinson—the latter famously calling him "a walking museum" for his encyclopedic recall and Dodger pin collection. Allen had a strong connection later in life with Duke Snider as they ran into each other constantly at Sports Collectors Conventions from the

Boson area to the Asbury Park Convention Center and as far west as the Allentown, Pennsylvania area.

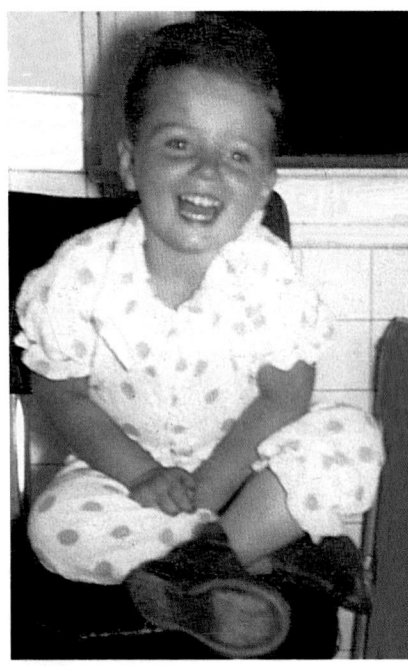

Allen at about age three just barely had a grasp of the Dodgers, but that soon changed and has been constant for nearly three quarters of a Century.

Trained as an archaeologist and anthropologist, Schery combines rigorous historical scholarship with philosophical insight across an impressive body of writing. His groundbreaking research in "The Boys of Spring: The Birth of the Dodgers" unearthed the team's founding corporate records dating back to 1883, overturning long-held myths by revealing the involvement of wealthy gamblers as key founders. His follow-up, "Brooklyn Dodgers at Ebbets Field 1913-1957", chronicles five vibrant decades of Dodger culture, capturing the essence of the team's golden era through vivid storytelling and deep archival exploration.

Beyond baseball history, Schery's intellectual pursuits span multiple disciplines. His prolific works include The Shattered Cross-The Rise, Fall, and Undying Legacy of the Knights Templars, a richly detailed examination of medieval history blending mystery and scholarship; The Mystery of the Ark, an ambitious narrative steeped in speculative history and religious lore based on the style of Dan Brown; and The Pattern Seeking Ape, a philosophical exploration of human cognition, culture, and the ceaseless human drive to find meaning.

As a museum designer and curator, Schery's visionary talents have shaped notable cultural institutions. He created and curated the award-winning Corvette Americana Museum in Cooperstown, New York, recognized among New York's top museums in 1994 alongside giants like the Met and Guggenheim. In Los Angeles, recruited by Dodgers executive Tommy Hawkins, he helped design and curate the Dodger Experience Museum at Dodger Stadium to showcase his unrivaled collection. Currently, he has completed designed plans for an ambitious 46,000-square-foot Dodger Museum that will recreate the historic ballparks the Dodgers have played in as immersive environments using decades of collectibles to shape each room. Allen also played a pivotal role in assembling the Rose Bowl Museum exhibits, designing a $200,000 project showcasing the 110-year history of the Rose Parade and nearly a century of football at the stadium. The Rose Bowl displays history not merely of sport but as a window into American culture, featuring memorabilia, photographs, and trophies assembled from private donors and institutional collections.

Operating under his Brooklyn Bridge Books imprint, Allen blends research, writing, and curation to illuminate themes spanning sports history, archaeology, anthropology, philosophy, and human experience. His interdisciplinary vision challenges conventional boundaries, inviting readers and audiences to engage deeply with history's nuances, whether tracing medieval orders, ancient quests for sacred relics, or the cultural heartbeat of America's pastime.

For over seventy years, Schery's dedication to preserving and interpreting the past—whether through scholarly books, museum exhibits, or personal mentorship—has made him a uniquely influential figure in his fields. Based in Los Angeles for the last 25 years, his work continues to bridge ancient civilizations, modern culture, and the universal human story, inspiring both scholarly inquiry and popular fascination in the style of Carl Sagan who he met in the early 1970's at Cornell University. By the end of the year Allen will publish four additional books. The next one which is finished and in production is called "The Primate Principal-Why Chimps and Humans steal bananas". Others will be on the Illuminati, the Papacy and a third on Philosophy being a human "Mind Painting". There are also plans for a Viking history book along with one on Thoreau and Emerson. Also in the works is a book on President James Monroe. As you can see Allen has a broad interest in Social Science and Humanities topics. He feels that once one learns logic and the scientific method and how to research-anything goes. He will not tackle Physics, Chemistry or Calculus. He feels that there are eighty-eight keys on the piano and will explore as many as possible.

Additional pictures of Allen's Dodger Collection

Contents

1. The Brooklyn Heartbreak & The Visionary's Imperative (The Prelude to Migration) — 1
2. Arrival and Immediate Concerns — 13
3. The Inaugural Season in L.A.: A Tumultuous Welcome and the Coliseum's Grip — 29
4. The Maury Wills Story — 49
5. The Cinderella Story: How the '59 Pennant Was Won. — 63
6. A World Series for a New Home: Triumph in the City of Angels featuring Fairfax High School Heroes Larry Sherry and Chuck Essegian. — 81
7. The Hangover Effect: The Challenges of Defending a Title 1960. — 99
8. The Hangover Lingers, But the Future Beckons The 1961 Season: A Near Miss — 114
9. The Challenges of Building Dodger Stadium — 139
10. The Pioneers of the New Frontier — 161

11.	The Opening of Dodger Stadium and the heartbreak of 1962.	174
12.	The Unforgettable Sweep: How the 1963 Dodgers Conquered the Yankees	203
Bibliography		229
Endnotes		245

Chapter One

The Brooklyn Heartbreak & The Visionary's Imperative (The Prelude to Migration)

For generations, Ebbets Field had been more than just a ballpark; it was the sacred, beating heart of Brooklyn, a cozy, intimate cathedral where the Dodgers, affectionately known as "Dem Bums," played a brand of baseball woven inextricably into the borough's working-class fabric. The air seemed to hum with its loyal fans' collective hopes and frustrations, a place where legends like Jackie Robinson and Duke Snider took root. But by the mid-1950s, the beloved charm of Ebbets Field was eroding into acute disrepair. Its grand façade, once proud, showed cracks of neglect; its antiquated infrastructure struggled to handle modern crowds; and its capacity, peaking at around 32,000, was woefully inadequate for growing attendance demands. For instance, on many popular game days, thousands of fans were turned away, leading to estimated revenue losses of over $500,000 per season, a significant sum for the era. The restrooms were often overflowing and unsanitary, concession stands were few and far between, leading to long lines, and structural elements like concrete supports showed visible spalling and cracking.

Beyond parking, the very design of Ebbets Field, with its cramped concourse space, limited restroom facilities, and lack of modern amenities like luxury boxes, severely restricted revenue streams from concessions and other fan services. These limitations meant the Dodgers' profitability lagged behind teams in newer venues, hindering Walter O'Malley's ability to invest in the team and compete effectively. O'Malley, the Dodgers' insightful owner, understood with cold clarity that the future of professional sports demanded more than just nostalgic reverence. He envisioned a modern, profitable enterprise, a sprawling, fan-friendly complex that Ebbets Field simply couldn't be. A new, state-of-the-art stadium was not merely a luxury but an economic imperative to ensure the Dodgers could compete and thrive. O'Malley's ultimate goal was clear: to own a modern, profitable stadium and the surrounding land, creating a long-term asset that would guarantee the franchise's financial stability and competitive edge for decades to come, much like the Yankees benefited from their ownership of Yankee Stadium. Another concern rarely mentioned was that the Braves moving to Milwaukee saw an increase in attendance that could not be matched in tiny Ebbets Field.

July, 1957 Sport magazine shows artwork by famous illustrator John Cullen Murphy shows aging Ebbets Field (top), Dodger Manager Walter Alston and Dodger President O'Malley (center), flanked on the left by Dodger shortstop Pee Wee Reese and on the right by Dodger center fielder Duke Snider and a rendering of a new dome stadium for the Dodgers in Brooklyn (bottom). The original illustration was given to O'Malley.

O'Malley's persistent and increasingly earnest attempts to secure a new home in Brooklyn were not merely met with indifference, but actively complicated by the monolithic power of Robert Moses. New York City's unparalleled master builder and parks commissioner, Moses, wielded significant, almost unchecked, authority over public land and infrastructure, driven by his grand, often uncompromising, vision for urban redevelopment.

O'Malley presented multiple detailed proposals, including an ambitious plan for a domed stadium at the strategic intersection of Atlantic and Flatbush Avenues. This potentially revolutionary, multi-purpose facility promised to enhance the fan experience and spark significant urban renewal in the borough.

Yet, Moses, seeing private enterprise potentially conflicting with his public works agenda, systematically dismissed O'Malley's initiatives. The core of their conflict lay in O'Malley's insistence on private land ownership for the stadium versus Moses's unwavering belief that public land should remain under public control and that private entities should not profit from its development. Moses famously declared he would not "tear down the city for a ballpark," viewing O'Malley's desire for land ownership as an affront to his public domain philosophy and a perceived demand for a "subsidy," even when O'Malley, sought only infrastructure improvements and eminent domain assistance, not outright cash for construction. O'Malley had sold Ebbets Field in

Brooklyn and a Montreal stadium to raise millions to invest in the new Brooklyn stadium for the Dodgers. He would also have added a year-round parking structure to benefit Brooklyn and eliminate a highly congested area with his multipurpose domed stadium. Moses fundamentally believed that a sports stadium, while a public amenity, should not be the catalyst for the city to transfer valuable public land to a private entity, especially when it might divert resources from his grander, city-wide public works projects.

Robert Moses self-righteous arrogance was the main reason for the Dodgers leaving Brooklyn.

While Moses consistently promoted a site in Flushing Meadows, Queens, as the desirable alternative, O'Malley viewed this as too distant from the core Brooklyn fan base, inconveniently located for access, and lacking the necessary transit and parking infrastructure without massive, publicly funded development, which Moses was unwilling to provide for a private entity. The Flushing Meadows site, while vast, was largely undeveloped marshland that would have required extensive landfill and new subway lines to make it viable for large crowds, costs Moses expected O'Malley to bear entirely for a private venture, unlike the public funds he readily allocated for his own projects. Moses also dismissed numerous other suggestions from various parties in Brooklyn. These included sites in Coney Island (the Luna Park area), which Moses deemed too isolated and already earmarked for public recreational development; Fort Greene Park, which was a historic green space Moses protected fiercely; Gerritsen Beach, too remote and requiring extensive infrastructure development; and Staten Island, which O'Malley dismissed due to poor transit links and fan access. Even a proposal to convert the Parade Grounds in Prospect Park into a professional ballpark, despite being championed by City Council President Abe Stark, was met with public outcry over displacing youth sports and practical concerns about traffic and neighborhood disruption. Moses's firm stance and priorities for urban planning, which often favored massive public works and car-centric infrastructure over subway access to Brooklyn,

One thing never mentioned is that Walter O'Malley's entire essence was New York. Whether it be the Bronx, Hollis, Amityville, Brooklyn, his wife and children, fishing tournaments, businesses owned (New York Subways Advertising, J.P. Duffy Co., maker of building materials), board of directorships (Brooklyn Gas Co. and others), business associates, and a decade-long proven track record of trying to keep the Dodgers in Brooklyn, how likely would it be that he pulls a red herring like Los Angeles out of his hat? All the discourse and false narrative hinged over only one thing, his non-acceptance of Flushing Meadows as an alternative for his new home. O'Malley wanted to privately build and own the park and avoid paying rent. Once, New York power broker Robert Moses had the soundbite of rejection he kept pounding the table and quoting it. It finally became cemented in the minds of locals with the birth of the New York Mets, and Shea Stadium in the same Flushing Meadows O'Malley turned down. The assuming of the Dodgers and Giants colors for the Mets was the last nail in this erstwhile coffin. Meanwhile, through all this, Walter O'Malley was 3000 miles away and too busy to be involved in a one-sided conversation he never wanted.

A radically different landscape of opportunity was beckoning. Los Angeles, a sprawling, vibrant metropolis experiencing an unprecedented post-war boom, presented an inviting alternative to Brooklyn's stagnancy. Brooklyn itself, during this period, faced growing economic challenges and a shifting population base, making O'Malley's vision for growth increasingly difficult to realize locally. Manufacturing jobs were declining, many middle-class families were moving to the suburbs, and the borough's infrastructure was aging. Los Angeles, by contrast, was a city without a major league baseball team, yet overflowing with a rapidly expanding population, a booming economy, and an eager appetite for entertainment. Its post-war growth was fueled by industries like aerospace, film, and tourism, drawing millions seeking new opportunities and a different way of life.

Roz Wyman, a tenacious and visionary young city councilwoman, was at the forefront of this courtship. Elected at just 22, Wyman was convinced that for Los Angeles to truly achieve "big league" status, it needed major professional sports. She actively initiated correspondence with O'Malley as early as 1955, tirelessly working alongside Mayor Norris Poulson and County Supervisor Kenneth Hahn to demonstrate Los Angeles's eagerness and capability to host a team. This aggressive pursuit paid off when Wyman was instrumental in convincing O'Malley to visit Los Angeles in May 1957. During this crucial visit, aboard a two-seat helicopter tour orchestrated by city officials, O'Malley himself reportedly spotted Chavez Ravine—a vast, bowl-shaped expanse of undeveloped land northeast of downtown—recognizing its immense potential as the ideal site for his dream stadium. This bird's-eye perspective offered O'Malley the clear space, rugged hilly land that no one had previously been willing to tackle. But he envisioned carving into it by moving millions of cubic yards of earth to create the gentle slopes perfect for ample terraced parking, the geographical contours that Brooklyn had so stubbornly denied him, and the tantalizing promise of land ownership.

On May 2, 1957, Dodger owner Walter O'Malley takes a 50-minute helicopter ride to view prospective sites for Dodger Stadium. He claimed he was never so scared. Picture procured over 60 years ago by Author and part of Dodger Museum Collection.

Essentially, Los Angeles also offered the use of the massive Los Angeles Memorial Coliseum as a temporary home, mitigating the immediate stadium crisis. This was a critical concession, as it allowed O'Malley to move the team without having to wait years for a new stadium to be built. Adding to the strategic pressure was the looming threat of the "Continental League", a new, independent major league that might emerge if existing MLB teams didn't establish a West Coast presence. Such a league would not only siphon off talent but also threaten the financial stability and national dominance of Major League Baseball, a risk O'Malley, as a forward-thinking owner, was keen to avert. Importantly, National League owners had unanimously voted to approve O'Malley and New York Giants owner Horace Stoneham that both teams, facing similar stadium woes and the need to establish a viable West Coast presence, must move in tandem to California. This joint move was critical for the viability of West Coast baseball, making road trips for other National League teams economically feasible by offering two West Coast stops instead of just one, ensuring the preservation of their historic rivalry.

The final decision, made carefully in boardroom discussions, sent significant national ripples. For Brooklyn, it was a profound, deeply felt loss, a collective heartbreak whose effects lingered for generations. The news, when it finally broke, was met with stunned disbelief and a sense of betrayal among the intensely loyal fan base, who saw their team as an extension of their very identity. All of this betrayal can be laid at the feet of Robert Moses. The last games at Ebbets Field were steeped in a palpable melancholy as loyal fans grappled with the unfathomable departure of their beloved Bums, a betrayal that felt intensely personal. Even the players, caught amid the monumental change, felt the immense emotional weight of leaving behind their familiar lives for the vast, unknown expanse of the West Coast. The New York press, echoing the borough's strong emotions, often criticized O'Malley, portraying him as someone who prioritized business over community loyalty. Yet, in the complex tapestry of historical truth, it was ultimately the unyielding nature of Robert Moses's urban planning vision and his refusal to facilitate a viable, privately owned stadium solution in New York, coupled with the foresight and welcoming hand extended by figures like Roz Wyman and the transformative promise revealed from a helicopter ride over Chavez Ravine, that set the Dodgers on their course—from the foundations of a Brooklyn left behind, O'Malley, guided by necessity following his extraordinary decade long effort to keep the Dodgers in Brooklyn and a clear vision, prepared to embark on a significant venture in sports history, a journey not just across a continent, but into the uncharted territory of a new identity and a new destiny. This foundational deadlock in Brooklyn would not only reshape a city but fundamentally alter the landscape of American professional sports for decades to come, setting a precedent for future franchise relocations and the very notion of a "major league" presence across a vast continent.

ALLEN SCHERY

October 23, 1957, the Dodger-owned Convair 440 Metropolitan airplane arrives at LAX with Dodger President Walter O'Malley (middle) on the steps welcomed by Los Angeles County Supervisor Kenneth Hahn and Los Angeles City Councilmember Roz Wyman. A large crowd was on the tarmac to support the Dodgers arrival.

Chapter Two
Arrival and Immediate Concerns

The arrival of the Dodgers in Los Angeles in 1958 marked a significant moment for both the team and the city, though it was not without its challenges. The bold move from Brooklyn, and the subsequent efforts to establish a permanent home, involved intricate political maneuvering, spirited public debate, and necessary temporary solutions. The Dodgers' official arrival in Los Angeles occurred on October 23, 1957, when their Convair 440 Metropolitan team plane, newly emblazoned with "Los Angeles" on its side, touched down at the airport. Thousands of enthusiastic fans, eager for a taste of major league baseball, greeted them, a clear indication of the city's anticipation. This widespread excitement was equally reflected by local sportswriters and downtown businesses. This civic enthusiasm was further amplified by a major welcoming party held at the Statler Hotel on October 28, attended by a packed ballroom of 1,100 fans. During this event, Dodgers owner Walter O'Malley expressed his profound gratitude to the city, emphasizing the "grass-roots movement" of support that he felt "at every turn — on the streets, in the cabs, all over the city," and reiterated the team's unwavering commitment to the community, promising that "there never will be a time when anyone connected with the Dodgers will have to apologize for his conduct." However, this initial welcome was not entirely smooth, as dissidents vehemently opposed to the city's contract for the Chavez Ravine land served O'Malley with a summons upon his arrival, an early indication of the legal and political challenges that lay ahead. Immediately upon their arrival, O'Malley diligently began evaluating suitable playing fields, with the Rose Bowl in Pasadena, Wrigley Field in Los Angeles (the former home of the Pacific Coast League's Los Angeles Angels), and the venerable Los Angeles Memorial Coliseum being the primary contenders. Negotiations for the Rose Bowl as a temporary home ultimately fell through. On January 13, 1958, O'Malley and Pasadena City Manager Don C. McMillan jointly announced the failure of these negotiations, citing the prohibitive estimated minimum cost of $750,000 to convert the Rose Bowl for baseball, along with the "physical scars" it would leave on the "beautiful Rose Bowl." Furthermore, the Rose Bowl's distance from downtown Los Angeles and its limited public transit access were significant drawbacks. Obviously, the solution was not at hand and in a way mirrored the type of problems O'Malley saw in Brooklyn. Nothing there found an easy solution. Los Angeles was no different. More work was needed.

October 23, 1957, the Dodger-owned Convair 440 Metropolitan plane has just arrived at Los Angeles International Airport and is welcomed by a large crowd on the tarmac. Dodger President Walter O'Malley stands at the bottom of the stair ramp with Los Angeles Councilmember Roz Wyman in a long coat and Los Angeles County Supervisor Kenneth Hahn wearing a baseball cap.

Adding to this, on December 19, 1957, National League President Warren Giles had explicitly expressed concerns, stating that playing a "substantial number of your home games" outside Los Angeles city limits (as Pasadena was) could jeopardize the Dodgers' claim to the Los Angeles territory and potentially leave it "open" for another club to move in. The National League, having just approved the unprecedented dual West Coast move, was particularly keen to ensure the Los Angeles market was firmly established and protected, adding pressure on O'Malley to find a suitable, in-city solution without delay.

January 6, 1958, (L-R): Pasadena City Manager Don C. McMillan, Pasadena Asst. City Manager Robert McCurdy, National League President Warren C. Giles, and Dodger President Walter O'Malley meet regarding the possibility of using the famed Rose Bowl for 1958 Dodger home games. O'Malley was exploring options, such as the Los Angeles Memorial Coliseum and team-owned Wrigley Field in L.A.

Reluctantly, O'Malley then considered his own property, Wrigley Field, for the 1958 season. While located within Los Angeles, its capacity of 22,000 seats (expandable to only 23,600 with alterations) was a considerable downgrade from Ebbets Field's nearly 32,000, and its severe lack of parking (only 800 spaces at the park, with makeshift peripheral spaces on homeowners' lawns) was a significant drawback, mirroring a persistent issue O'Malley had faced in Brooklyn. O'Malley explicitly stated his unwillingness to "take a step backward" by settling for such a small venue, particularly given the essential need for a grand, modern stadium for the franchise's future. The Los Angeles Memorial Coliseum eventually emerged as O'Malley's chosen temporary solution, a plan famously conceived as his "3 a.m. Plan." This epiphany struck O'Malley in the early hours of January 17, 1958, after exhausting days of failed negotiations for the Rose Bowl and finding Wrigley Field unacceptable. He was reportedly immersed in his troubles instead of sleeping, acutely aware that the Dodgers, having publicly committed to Los Angeles, were on the verge of a national embarrassment if a suitable playing field within city limits couldn't be secured immediately. The "3 a.m. Plan" wasn't a long-considered strategy but a last-ditch, desperate inspiration to make the 100,000-seat Coliseum—a venue previously thought impractical for baseball—work through creative and extensive modifications.

Despite its primary use for football and other events, the Coliseum offered a much larger seating capacity, though it required wide-ranging and inventive modifications for baseball. These included the crucial erection of a 42-foot-high, removable screen in left field due to an absurdly short 251-foot distance down the line, adding a press box area in the stands, new dugouts, and three additional banks of lights to accommodate night games. Foul territory would also be considerable in some areas, and the diamond was to be located on the west end of the Coliseum without removing any of its physical properties. O'Malley also pledged a substantial rental fee of $300,000 per annum, which was then the highest ever paid by a baseball club. Despite these significant challenges and the sacrifice of typically lucrative home dates, including the Fourth of July, to accommodate traditional Coliseum tenants, the Dodgers were prepared to make it work.

The first game in Los Angeles was played at the Coliseum on April 18, 1958, with the Dodgers beating the San Francisco Giants 6-5 before a major league record crowd of 78,672. Dodger pitcher Ed Roebuck famously described the temporary home as "Grand Canyon with seats," a sentiment echoed by many players. For the team, adjusting to the Coliseum's unconventional dimensions was a significant challenge; the incredibly short left field (251 feet) favored right-handed pull hitters, while the cavernous right-center field (440 feet) became a power alley graveyard for lefties like

Duke Snider, whose home run numbers plummeted in 1958. Pitchers, too, struggled with the unpredictable nature of the Coliseum, with some finding it unsettling to pitch with the towering left-field screen so close. O'Malley, however, stoutly defended the Coliseum, stating it was "a better ballpark than the Polo Grounds and it's better than Ebbets Field" in terms of playing area, acknowledging its temporary nature and the fans' acceptance of it, largely due to the excitement brought on by the screen. Despite the high attendance figures, the immediate financial impact of playing in the Coliseum was mixed. While gate receipts were robust due to the sheer volume of fans, the substantial rental fees, costly modifications, and the loss of prime dates meant that the team's operating profits during these temporary years were often thinner than anticipated, underscoring O'Malley's continued efforts for a permanent, privately owned stadium that could truly capitalize on the market's potential and fulfill his "economic imperative." On May 26, 1958, O'Malley issued a lengthy press release, meticulously detailing the Dodgers' good faith actions and substantial financial commitments since their move west. These included the payment of $450,000 to the Pacific Coast League for the privilege of moving, $600,000 in round figures for a two-year lease at the Coliseum (receiving no parking fees there), $300,000 spent on converting the Coliseum for temporary baseball use, plus another $50,000 for its restoration for other events. Assembling his dream had way too many moving parts. More was to come!

Opening Day 1958 begins Dodgers four year run (1958-1961) at the Coliseum.

Crucially, he highlighted the commitment to build a $12,000,000 stadium at Chavez Ravine entirely with private funds, covering all excess costs for grading and interior roads—a significant point of distinction, as he noted that "All other major league stadia since have been built with taxpayers' money on tax-exempt property." With delays and all costs tallied, the actual Dodger Stadium price tag was $23 million. Furthermore, the Dodgers committed to donating to the City of Los Angeles a $500,000 Youth Recreation Center for twenty years, with an annual financial support of $60,000, and to turning over to the City of Los Angeles Wrigley Field (land, stadium, equipment, and lights), which had been appraised in 1957 at $2,250,000 by the city. The Dodgers had originally purchased Wrigley Field and the Angels franchise for $3,000,000.

Fulfilling the terms of the Dodgers – City of Los Angeles contract, the Dodgers paid for two baseball fields in the recreation area which opened across the street from the Police Academy adjacent to Dodger Stadium in the mid-1960s. In December, 1971, Los Angeles Mayor Sam Yorty approved an amendment to the city's maintenance-improvement agreement with the Dodgers enabling the city to receive three annual payments in advance totaling $180,000, less discount. The city needed the funds to purchase materials and supplies for Phase I of the Elysian Park water system. In addition, the city greatly benefited by moving the payments forward as it then "qualified to receive $477,286 in Emergency Employment Act funds to create 78 new jobs for the planning and installing of the water system." Mayor Yorty said, "We are grateful to Mr. Peter O'Malley, president of the Dodger organization, for his enthusiastic cooperation in making this action possible." According to the Los Angeles Sentinel, "Yorty noted that under the terms of the existing agreement with the Dodger organization, the city has been receiving an annual payment of $60,000 for maintenance or improvement of recreational facilities since 1962." O'Malley's dream was like a jigsaw puzzle that kept adding more complicated, moving parts. Everyone seemed to have an agenda. There was no way he could have conceived of these endless distractions. It required myriad adaptations and reworking of plans. It is amazing he got it done at all! As soon as one problem was solved up popped another one.

ALLEN SCHERY

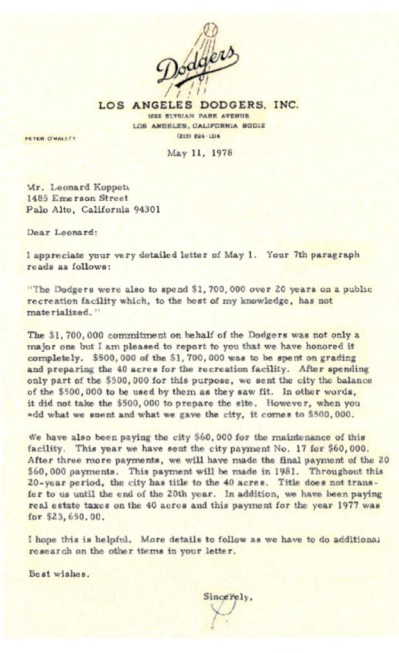

In a May 11, 1978 letter to author Leonard Koppett, Dodger President Peter O'Malley wrote about the recreational facilities, "The $1,700,000 commitment on behalf of the Dodgers was not only a major one but I am pleased to report to you that we have honored it completely...$500,000 of the $1,700,000 was to be spent on grading and preparing the 40 acres for the recreation facility. After spending only part of the $500,000 for this purpose, we sent the city the balance of the $500,000 to be used by them as they saw fit. This year we have sent the city payment No. 17 for $60,000. After three more payments, we will have made the final payment of the 20 $60,000 payments. This payment will be made in 1981. Throughout this 20-year period, the city has title to the 40 acres. Title does not transfer to us until the end of the 20th year. In addition, we have been paying real estate taxes on the 40 acres and this payment for the year 1977 was for $23,650.00."

Jim Hadaway, General Manager of the City of Los Angeles Department of Recreation and Parks from 1976-1992, contacted Peter O'Malley telling him that the fields were rarely being used and asked if the Dodgers would prepay the remaining years so that the city would have better use of those funds. O'Malley accommodated their request. The Dodgers then received title to the land and added more parking at Dodger Stadium.

An Associated Press poll published on May 24, 1958, showed "No on Proposition B" slightly ahead at 44.7% to 4 3.3%, with 12% undecided, indicating the close nature of the impending vote. To garner crucial support, the Dodgers and their allies launched a massive communication effort, leveraging all available means. On Sunday, June 1, 1958, as the Dodgers completed a road trip in Chicago, a live, five-hour "Dodgerthon" was held on KTTV Channel 11 in support of the contract and O'Malley's new stadium. This jam-packed lineup featured civic leaders, a host of celebrities (including Jerry Lewis, Ronald Reagan, George Burns, Dean Martin, Jack Benny, Laraine Day, Debbie Reynolds, Ray Walston, Casey Stengel, and Jackie Robinson via tape), and sports stars. The culmination of the show was the Dodgers' arrival on their team-owned Convair plane at Los Angeles International Airport's United Airlines terminal before thousands of adoring fans who surged onto the tarmac to greet their hometown heroes. The next night, O'Malley made his key points for supporting Proposition B on local television (Channel 13), while on the same show, his opponent J.A. Smith (who owned the San Diego Padres baseball club and was a significant financier of the referendum petition) presented opposing viewpoints. The "Proposition B" referendum vote took place on June 3, 1958, and resulted in the largest non-Presidential election turnout in Los Angeles history, with 62.3 percent of the city's 1,105,427 registered voters casting ballots.

He proudly broke ground for Dodger Stadium on September 17, 1959, holding a shovel alongside Supervisor Hahn, his son Jimmy Hahn (designated as the Dodger batboy and future Mayor of L.A.), Mayor Poulson, City Councilman Gordon Hahn, Dodger Vice President, Stadium Operations Dick Walsh, and members of the architectural and construction teams, including engineer and designer Capt. Emil Praeger. Praeger was a senior partner of the New York City firm Praeger, Kavanagh and Waterbury, and a distinguished Navy captain with an impeccable record as an authority on bridges, foundations, and parkways. He had previously been the consulting engineer for the structural and foundation design for the White House renovation in 1949 and provided his first stadium design for the Dodgers' 5,000-seat Holman Stadium project in 1952-53. Praeger, much like O'Malley, was a meticulous stickler for details, famously stating, "Skimp on the little things and the big thing won't be a success. That's engineering." This marked one of the proudest moments of O'Malley's life, as he knew his stadium dream would finally be realized. Despite all this glad handing achieving all this was no cakewalk. There were too many factions that wanted to be heard demanding an accounting of their concerns. Given the human experience in general this should not be a surprise. O'Malley needed to stay focused and alert. He probably needed a flak jacket but did not know it!

Dignitaries at the September 17, 1959 Dodger Stadium Groundbreaking Ceremonies included (L-R) City Councilman Gordon Hahn; Jack Yount, Vice President and on-site manager in charge of construction for Vinnell Constructors; County Supervisor Kenneth Hahn and his son Jimmy (who was honorary batboy and years later elected as Mayor of L.A.); C. Don "Arch" Field of the City Department of Public Works; Dodger President Walter O'Malley; and Al Vinnell of Vinnell Constructors.

While the stadium was under construction, the Los Angeles Dodgers truly embraced their new hometown, and Los Angelenos embraced them with gusto. While the 1958 Dodgers had trouble getting out of the gate, Major League Baseball was gaining widespread acceptance in its new environs, due in large part to the efforts of one man: Vin Scully. Scully's colorful descriptions and the widespread adoption of the transistor radio were catalysts for bringing fans to the Coliseum—and later to Dodger Stadium. Sitting high up in the Coliseum, often 80-plus rows above the action, Dodger fans relied on Scully's eloquent call of the game to tell them what was happening, even when they were at the game itself. It was later famously said, "Unless Vin Scully tells us that it happened, it didn't happen!" This profound trust in a broadcaster by the fans contributed to his Hall of Fame career of 67 seasons. But it also speaks volumes about Scully's extraordinary ability to woo families and especially women to the ballpark. If a listener did not understand the nuances of the game, Scully taught the fan with his poetic descriptions and storytelling style. The Dodgers, under O'Malley's ownership, always welcomed families to the stadia, but Scully was a large part of bringing those families back, time and time again. His impressive power of voice made him Southern California's most known, respected, and loved radio personality. The vast number of people who brought radios to the Coliseum, and later to Dodger Stadium, meant that a fan could walk anywhere throughout the stadium and parking lots and Vin

Scully's mellifluous voice could be heard. Of course, Scully's partner Jerry Doggett, who joined the Brooklyn Dodgers in 1956, was also extremely popular and perfectly complemented Scully. O'Malley himself stated, "People ask me, 'who is the greatest Dodger?' It's Scully. You know we hired him right out of school." Scully's loyalty to O'Malley and his family was rewarded for nearly half a century. Scully also recounted that O'Malley "always said if the Dodgers had lost that (day) game (on June 1, 1958) it would have influenced the referendum voting back in Los Angeles...He truly felt winning that game helped win the referendum." Initially, O'Malley and the Dodgers did not plan to air road games on local television, but he decided on April 27, 1958, to place all away games from San Francisco on KTTV Channel 11 beginning with the May 9 game, marking the beginning of a longtime partnership that lasted for 34 years. Vin Scully cut his teeth way back in Ebbets Field, Brooklyn, where he wooed the fans with his "word wonderment". His style resembled Grantland Rice's Pre-Radio and Television technique where adjectives and adverbs added "color". He developed his own unique style using such terms as deuces wild when there were two on two out and a count of 2 and 2. The fans loved this as well as they loved him. He became a cherished fixture. Vin Scully saw induction into the National Baseball Hall of Fame in 1982, recognizing his significant contributions to baseball broadcasting. His induction was a testament to his impact on the sport and his ability to connect with fans through his storytelling and commentary. Scully's induction into the Hall of Fame was a fitting tribute to his long and distinguished career, which included calling various nationally televised sports events and being a beloved figure in the broadcasting community. He is truly missed by all the fans.

Peter O'Malley (left) and his dad Walter O'Malley, circa 1952 spring training, point out the Dodger logo on the Douglas DC-3 airplane, which was in service from 1950 until the arrival of the Convair 440 in 1957.

Chapter Three

The Inaugural Season in L.A.: A Tumultuous Welcome and the Coliseum's Grip

The 1958 season opened with a profound sense of uncertainty and an almost surreal atmosphere for the Los Angeles Dodgers. While the monumental crowds at the Los Angeles Memorial Coliseum were undoubtedly thrilling, often exceeding 70,000 spectators and shattering attendance records, this electrifying reception starkly contrasted with the reality of the team on the field. This was largely a shadow of the Brooklyn powerhouse that had captured the hearts of a borough and won a World Series just three years prior. The once vibrant core of that championship team was visibly aging, its collective star fading. Several key figures, who had been integral to Brooklyn's success, were either well past their athletic prime, sidelined by nagging injuries, or simply no longer with the organization. Pee Wee Reese, for instance, was nearing the end of his illustrious career, his once-swift legs slowing, while the devastating car accident of Roy Campanella just months before the season began left an irreparable void behind the plate.

On April 18, 1958, the opening day of the Los Angeles Dodgers at the Los Angeles Memorial Coliseum, the attendance was 78,672 fans, which was a record crowd at the time. This event marked the beginning of the Dodgers' successful run in Los Angeles, and the Coliseum became a significant venue for the team.

The seismic move west marked not merely a dramatic change of address for the franchise, relocating over 3,000 miles, but also heralded a significant and often painful transitional period for the roster itself, caught between a glorious past and an uncertain future. The team finished its inaugural season in the National League with a deeply disappointing

71-83 record, placing them in a dismal seventh place, a full 21 games behind the pennant-winning Milwaukee Braves. This disheartening on-field performance served as a stark, immediate reminder that simply relocating to a new, eager city did not automatically translate to continued or immediate success. The magic of Brooklyn, it seemed, had not traveled intact across the continent.

The Dodgers' first regular-season game in Los Angeles took place at the Memorial Coliseum on April 18, 1958, against the San Francisco Giants, drawing a record crowd of 78,672 fans. The Dodgers won this historic game 6–5 in a dramatic finish that involved memorable plays and errors, such as Jim Davenport missing third base on an apparent tying run in the ninth inning. The very first home run in Los Angeles Dodgers history was hit by Dick Gray in the second game of the season, and he also hit the first Dodger home run at the Coliseum in their inaugural home game. Popular Dodger right-handed pitcher Carl Erskine started the first major league game in Los Angeles and was the winning pitcher. "Oisk" as he was known in Brooklyn, had also started and won the first Dodger exhibition game played at Holman Stadium, Dodgertown, Vero Beach, Florida on March 11, 1953. Erskine pitched two no-hitters for the Dodgers as well as striking out a World Series record Yankees in the 1953 fall classic.

Gil Hodges hit his 300th career home run, and Pee Wee Reese played his 2,000th career game on the same day, both key personal achievements for veteran players. although the celebration was tempered by Snider's pregame arm injury, a harbinger of the physical struggles that would persist all year. Beyond these milestones, tragedy cast a pall over the team when Roy Campanella's offseason car accident left him paralyzed, ending his Hall of Fame career before he could ever take the field in Los Angeles. Don Newcombe, the former Cy Young and MVP winner, was traded to Cincinnati during the season after a rough start, which marked a significant roster change and indicated the end of an era for one of Brooklyn's stars. Other transactions included the sale of Randy Jackson to the Cleveland Indians and the addition of several other players.

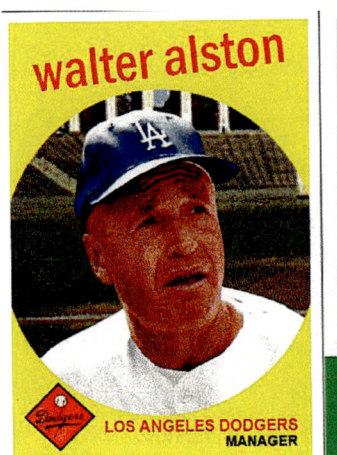

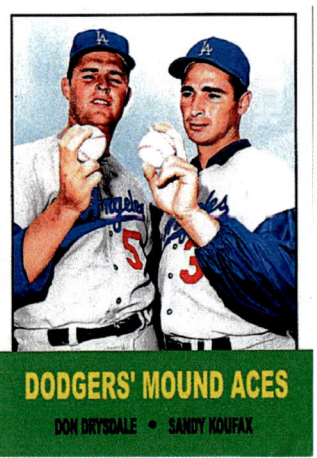

Walter Alston and Drysdale/Koufax cards from Author's Dodger Museum Collection.

Early Topps Los Angeles Dodgers Cards from Author's Dodger Museum Collection.

The Dodgers were welcomed with fanfare, including a parade down Broadway and a City Hall ceremony to mark the team's arrival in Los Angeles. Mayor Norris Poulson and owner Walter O'Malley played symbolic roles in welcoming the team.

Opening Day ceremonies Norris Poulson and Walter O'Malley

Fan excitement was significant, seen not only in crowd size but in civic ceremonies and the broader cultural impact of having Major League Baseball on the West Coast for the first time. Manager Walter Alston, renowned for his steady hand

and methodical baseball philosophy, found his skills tested and his strategies upended. The quirky dimensions of the Coliseum—especially its 251-foot left-field line contrasting with an expansive right-center at 440 feet—forced Alston to employ advanced platooning, focus on matchups dictated by handedness, and prioritize "small ball" tactics like bunting and hit-and-run plays. To cope with the stadium's predisposition to cheap home runs, especially for left-handed hitters, Alston leaned heavily on groundball pitching and strategic bullpen use, often bringing in reliever Clem Labine—who finished with a league-leading 14 saves—earlier in games than was typical for that era. Nevertheless, the peculiar ballpark exacted a mental and physical toll on pitchers such as Don Drysdale, whose ERA jumped as he surrendered a career-high in home runs, and on Sandy Koufax, who endured uneven development due to the stadium's punitive environment for left-handed power pitchers. Don Drysdale, the towering young flamethrower known for his intimidating inside fastball and fiery mound presence openly voiced his deep frustration with the "sideshow" dimensions, particularly the short left field, which he felt unjustly turned many well-pitched balls into cheap, demoralizing home runs. "You could make a great pitch, and it would just get a little high, and boom, it's out of here," Drysdale lamented, expressing a sentiment shared by many hurlers. While he finished with a seemingly respectable 12-13 record given the team's struggles, his earned run average ballooned to 4.17 (a sharp increase from his impressive 2.69 ERA in 1957), and he allowed 21 home runs, a career-high at that point in his burgeoning career. He started the season with a dismal 1-7 record, a clear and agonizing indication of his early struggles to adapt to the new pitching environment. Sandy Koufax, still in his early, unpolished career, also struggled significantly at the Coliseum in those nascent years. From 1958 through 1961, his home ERA and home run rates were considerably worse than his road numbers, starkly illustrating the ballpark's negative influence. He was 17-23 with a 4.33 ERA at home, allowing an alarming 56 home runs, compared to a far more respectable 28-20 record with a 3.57 ERA and 33 home runs allowed on the road. The short left-field porch was particularly detrimental to his powerful left-handed curveball, which could sometimes hang and be pulled easily by right-handed batters seeking a quick home run.

Even the former Cy Young winner and MVP from Brooklyn, Don Newcombe, struggled immensely in 1958. He began the season with a dismal 0-6 record and a 7.86 ERA in 11 appearances (8 starts) before mercifully being traded to the Cincinnati Reds on June 15, 1958. While his decline was multifaceted and perhaps already underway, the new and unfamiliar environment certainly did not help him regain a Hall of Fame form.

Despite these widespread struggles, some players, through sheer adaptability or unexpected fortune, found ways to succeed. While Wally Moon's iconic "Moon Shots" are most famously associated with the 1959 season (he was acquired by the Dodgers in December 1958 for Gino Cimoli and thus didn't play for the Dodgers in 1958), the glaring need for players who could specifically exploit the short left field became abundantly evident throughout the entire 1958 season. Moon would famously re-configure his swing in 1959 to hit high, arcing fly balls that became home runs over the imposing 42-foot screen, despite being mere pop-ups in virtually any other conventional ballpark. Charlie Neal, the Dodgers' second baseman, had a breakout year, hitting an impressive 22 home runs and driving in 65 RBIs from his position, a strong showing that undoubtedly benefited from the Coliseum's short left field, which perfectly suited his right-handed swing. Young catcher John Roseboro also showed surprising power, hitting 14 home runs and batting a respectable .271 in 114 games, indicating that some players, particularly those with a quick, compact swing, could indeed leverage the new, quirky dimensions to their advantage. Veteran Carl Furillo hit 18 home runs and led the team with 83 RBIs, proving that consistent contact and a disciplined approach could still produce effectively, with his right-field position and its more conventional depth perhaps better suiting his hitting style than the extreme conditions of the other outfield spots.

While the team navigated its on-field growing pains and adjusted to the challenges of the Coliseum, Walter O'Malley, the Dodgers' visionary and deeply committed owner, was tirelessly working behind the scenes to secure the franchise's long-term and stable future in Los Angeles. For O'Malley, 1958 was far more than just another season of baseball; it was a critical and relentless year dedicated to laying the intricate groundwork for his ultimate, ambitious vision: a privately financed, purpose-built stadium that would serve as the Dodgers' permanent home, a project he had already envisioned for years in Brooklyn. His primary focus, consuming much of his energy and political capital, was the momentous Chavez Ravine land deal, an extraordinarily complex undertaking that would ultimately determine the site of their permanent home. The agreement to acquire the land for Dodger Stadium, which had been previously approved by the Los Angeles City Council after intense lobbying, faced significant and highly organized opposition from various fronts. Critics, often backed by labor unions and some progressive groups, vociferously argued against the use of public land for a private enterprise, especially when the area had once been slated for public housing projects. Opponents successfully gathered the required number of signatures to force a direct public referendum on the deal, cleverly branded as Proposition B, to be held on June 3, 1958. This vote was absolutely pivotal, as it would directly decide whether the city could proceed with conveying the contested land to the Dodgers. On May 26, 1958, O'Malley issued a lengthy statement which included, "We regret being in the throes of a political controversy instead of a contender in the National League race for the pennant. J.A. Smith testified he and his brother (C. Arnholt Smith) own the San Diego (Padres) Baseball Club (of the Pacific Coast League) and that he put up about 40% of the money to circulate the Referendum petition. His San Diego interest in keeping major league baseball out of Los Angeles is obvious. Without his contributions we probably never would have had the Referendum. As to the councilmen, they are public officials, and they voted on the matter. I regret that they want to second-guess the official vote of their body. We have kept every promise we made, and we know the city and county will do likewise. We will fight to stay in Los Angeles. There is neither the time nor the willingness on either side to renegotiate what is already a fair contract and suffer the chance of still another referendum. We have fulfilled and will fulfill all conditions of the contract – and are confident that the voters will want to do likewise." On November 5, 1957, James F. Mulvaney, President of the San Diego Padres, and former major leaguer Ralph Kiner, General Manager of the Padres, wrote a joint letter sent to O'Malley stating, "As we have previously told you, we have everything to lose and nothing to gain if the referendum is successful and, therefore, definitely have no interest, whatsoever, in its success."

Despite fierce and often bitter campaigning from both sides, characterized by heated public debates, extensive media coverage, and even a "Dodgerthon" telethon on KTTV that featured supporters including Jackie Robinson, Proposition B narrowly passed, by an incredibly slim margin of more than 25,000 votes out of over 677,000 cast. This razor-thin victory was, nonetheless, a monumental triumph for O'Malley, signaling a crucial segment of the public's overwhelming desire for the Dodgers to remain a permanent fixture in Los Angeles and clearing a massive political and legal hurdle for the eventual construction of Dodger Stadium. While legal challenges would inevitably continue for some time, the referendum's passage was an undeniable and crucial turning point that secured the team's future in the burgeoning metropolis.

Beyond the all-consuming land deal, O'Malley was actively and strategically involved in establishing the Dodgers as an indispensable fixture in the sprawling, car-centric Los Angeles market. He possessed a keen understanding of the unique nature of this new urban landscape and the essential need for the team to cultivate a broad and deep appeal across its diverse population. He was famously known for his unwavering commitment to keeping ticket prices genuinely affordable for families, a philosophy he maintained rigorously, holding prices between a mere 75 cents and $ 3.50 for 18 years (1958-1975) after the move, a remarkable feat in an era of rising costs. This policy was a deliberate counter to the perception of professional sports as an elite activity. O'Malley also made strategic, and prescient moves in broadcasting; on April 27, 1958, he made the significant announcement that the Dodgers would begin televising their remaining road games from San Francisco on KTTV Channel

11, reversing an earlier, more restrictive policy that limited broadcasts to avoid impacting gate attendance. This decision marked the beginning of a long-standing and highly successful partnership with the local television station and dramatically expanded the team's reach into Angelenos' homes, allowing more fans to connect with their new team, especially in a city built around the automobile and television. He also demonstrated foresight in recognizing the city's diverse population, diligently continuing and actively expanding the pioneering effort of Spanish-language radio broadcasts for games, a tradition that had actually begun in Brooklyn and now found an even larger, receptive audience in Southern California. His entire front office staff was rigorously instructed to be highly responsive and courteous to all fan inquiries, reflecting O'Malley's deep and personal commitment to exceptional customer service and fostering genuine community integration in what was, at first, an unfamiliar and challenging market. O'Malley viewed himself as an exceptionally hands-on owner, deeply and personally involved in virtually every facet of the business, from innovative marketing campaigns to meticulous facility planning aimed at ensuring the enduring long-term success, financial stability with a fine-tuned connection of the Los Angeles Dodgers to their new fan base. A tragic car accident to legendary catcher Roy Campanella in January 1958 left him paralyzed, prematurely ending his Hall of Fame career and robbing him of the chance to play a single game for the Los Angeles Dodgers.

His devastating absence left a massive and irreplaceable void in leadership, offensive production, and defensive prowess behind the plate. Campanella was universally beloved by fans and players alike for his infectious joy and powerful personality, and his injury cast a profound pall over the nascent Los Angeles era, serving as a constant reminder of what the team had lost. The subsequent massive tribute game held in his honor in 1959, attended by a record-breaking crowd that packed the Coliseum, was made all the more poignant by his inability to ever take the field for the team in their new home. Jackie Robinson, while famously retired after the 1956 season still loomed large in the team's broader legacy and the collective consciousness of the Brooklyn faithful. His groundbreaking impact on the Brooklyn Dodgers was foundational, not just for his electrifying play but for his courageous and transformative role in breaking baseball's color barrier, shattering racial segregation in professional sports. In 1958, he continued his vital work as a prominent spokesman and tireless fundraiser for the NAACP, serving as a powerful reminder of the ongoing social progress and moral leadership that had so profoundly defined the Brooklyn Dodgers' era.

Roy Campanella's Liquor store shortly before his tragic accident in Glen Cove.

His continued activism served as a subtle but notable contrast to the new, more commercialized and less overtly socially pioneering Los Angeles environment. Notably, on June 1, 1958, Robinson appeared via tape on the five-hour KTTV "Dodgerthon," lending his crucial support for Proposition B and vocally advocating for the city of Los Angeles' contract with the Dodgers, underscoring the enduring connection. Despite his strong public support for the move, his physical presence and unparalleled leadership were no longer in the clubhouse, another key, intangible element missing from the old, familiar team, leaving the 1958 squad searching for new voices and a new identity. Following the 1956 season, Jackie Robinson had made arrangements to announce in an exclusive article in Look magazine in January 1957 that he was retiring from baseball to work as director of personnel for Chock Full o'Nuts. Robinson was unable to share this news to protect the release of the story in the magazine. Unaware of the agreement between Look and Robinson, the Dodgers consummated a December 13, 1956, trade with the Giants, Robinson and pitcher Dick Littlefield being the principals. The Dodgers wanted to fulfill Robinson's desire to play for another team in New York, if he could not play for the Dodgers, thus the trade with the Giants. Both the Dodgers and Robinson were miffed, as the Dodgers said a trade would not have been made if they had known about Jackie's impending intentions to retire.

1952 Topps # 312. Impossible to find from Author's Dodger Museum Collection.

The story in Look was leaked January 8, 1957. When the Robinson article in Look came out on January 22, the Giants were still prepared to offer Robinson a contract, but by then Robinson had decided to voluntarily retire from baseball, invalidating the trade.

In essence, the 1958 season was undeniably a difficult but ultimately formative one for the Los Angeles Dodgers. The team was in a profound state of flux, attempting to find its new identity in a sprawling, unfamiliar city and adapting to the truly bizarre challenges of the Los Angeles Memorial Coliseum ballpark. While the crowds were massive and enthusiastic, creating an undeniable buzz, the on-field product was inconsistent, and individual players visibly wrestled with adjusting their unique games to the Coliseum's extreme peculiarities. The transition was not merely geographical but also psychological and strategic, a grand experiment played out nightly under the lights of a repurposed Olympic stadium. Yet, beneath the surface of the struggles and frustrations, Walter O'Malley's relentless efforts behind the scenes were diligently securing the foundational elements for the team's permanent and highly successful presence in Los Angeles. It was a year defined by learning curves, on-field struggles, and the painstaking laying of groundwork for the crucial adjustments that would eventually lead to their triumphant first Los Angeles championship in 1959, marking a true turning point for the franchise in its new, adopted home.

O'Malley successfully transitioned the Dodgers from Brooklyn to New York; found a temporary Los Angeles home for them to play in at the Coliseum after devising his "3 a.m. Plan"; fought off an unexpected ballot measure to Los Angeles voters designed to void the previously approved city contract with the Dodgers and other legal challenges; and opened a new market for Major League Baseball in Southern California. He established a Knothole Club program with thousands of free Dodger tickets distributed to youth. O'Malley hired Dr. Bob Woods and Dr. Robert Kerlan as team physicians, shaping a path that would later include highly-respected partner of Kerlan, Dr. Frank Jobe. In a March 24, 1958, article in Sports Illustrated, O'Malley expressed his continuing interest in Pay TV stating, "I think subscription TV will offer a solution to the problems that are plaguing many major sports. I'm not at all sure that the real baseball fan resents a modest price for subscription TV, free of commercials." One week after the Dodgers' 1958 season concluded, O'Malley proudly walked his daughter Terry down the aisle as she married Roland Seidler, Jr. The happy couple met at the Dodgers-Philadelphia Phillies on May 4, 1958, doubleheader at the Coliseum. Terry had worked as O'Malley's personal secretary upon their Los Angeles arrival. All of this happened in 1958 while O'Malley was laser-focused on his true goal – privately financing, building and maintaining a new 50,000-seat stadium for the Dodgers in Los Angeles as soon as possible.

ALLEN SCHERY

Walter O'Malley's final idea for new Dodger Ball Park

In January, 1958, Walter O'Malley devised his "3 a.m. Plan" on how to place a baseball diamond within the confines of the football-friendly Los Angeles Memorial Coliseum. The result was a short left field wall, 251 feet down the line, with a 40-foot-high screen to run far into left center field to reduce short distance home runs. The Coliseum had to be approved by the National League.

Chapter Four

The Maury Wills Story

Before the iconic 'Go! Go! Go!' chant echoed through Dodger Stadium, and long before he shattered baseball's most hallowed stolen base record, Maury Wills's journey began far from the bright lights of professional sports. His early life unfolded in the starkly segregated landscape of Washington D.C. Born Maurice Morning Wills on October 2, 1932, he was one of 13 children to Guy Wills, a sharecropper father who had migrated north from Georgia as part of the Great Migration, seeking opportunity. Growing up in the Anacostia neighborhood, a predominantly Black area, Wills's early life was deeply marked by the pervasive realities of racial segregation and economic hardship. Money was scarce, and resources were severely limited in their humble rowhouse on E Street SE, but the Wills household instilled in its children a fierce work ethic, a deep appreciation for family, and the enduring strength of community bonds.

Maury displayed innate athleticism from a young age, though baseball wasn't his singular focus; rather, it was one of many avenues for his boundless energy. He excelled in multiple sports at Cardozo High School, particularly football, where his quick decision-making and agility made him a star quarterback. He was also a standout in basketball and a talented track athlete, showcasing the raw speed, explosive acceleration, and unparalleled agility that would later define his professional career. He once ran the 100-yard dash in a blistering 9.5 seconds, a time that would impress even professional sprinters. Despite his undeniable prowess across various athletic fields, the path to a professional athletic career for a young Black man in the 1950s remained fraught with systemic obstacles. Opportunities were still significantly limited, even after Jackie Robinson had bravely broken baseball's color barrier just a few years prior, and the immense financial pressures on his large family meant that any dream of a sports career had to be carefully weighed against the immediate and pressing need for income to help support his siblings and parents.

It was baseball, however, that ultimately beckoned. In 1950, at 17, Wills signed his first professional contract with the Brooklyn Dodgers for a meager $500 bonus and $150 a month. This moment, seemingly a triumphant beginning, instead ushered in nearly a decade of grinding anonymity in the minor leagues. Wills crisscrossed the country for nine long seasons, accumulating 1,000 games and 4,000 at-bats for forgotten teams in places like Hornell, New York (Class D); Pueblo, Colorado (Class B); and Spokane, Washington (Triple-A). He battled the harsh realities of minor league life—meager pay that barely covered living expenses, endless and grueling bus rides on unpaved roads, and the soul-crushing uncertainty of whether he would ever reach the majors. During these formative years, he faced not only the intrinsic challenges of the game but also the insidious racism that persisted in many parts of the country, particularly in the Jim Crow South where some Dodger farm teams were located. Wills often experienced segregated accommodations, being denied service in restaurants, and enduring daily indignities and slights that only hardened his resolve and fueled his internal fire to succeed. He toiled for years as a third baseman, then a second baseman, and later, almost in desperation, taught himself to switch-hit, a crucial, career-saving move suggested by minor league manager Bobby Bragan. Without it, his career likely would have stalled permanently. Wills spent countless hours practicing his left-handed swing in front of a mirror, driven by pure necessity. Numerous times, frustration and despair nearly led him to quit baseball entirely, convinced his chance would never come. However, fueled by an internal fire and the profound lessons of perseverance learned from his humble beginnings, he refused to give up, tirelessly refining his skills, sharpening his instincts, and meticulously studying the game. He transformed his body into a finely tuned instrument, anticipating every pitch and every defensive move.

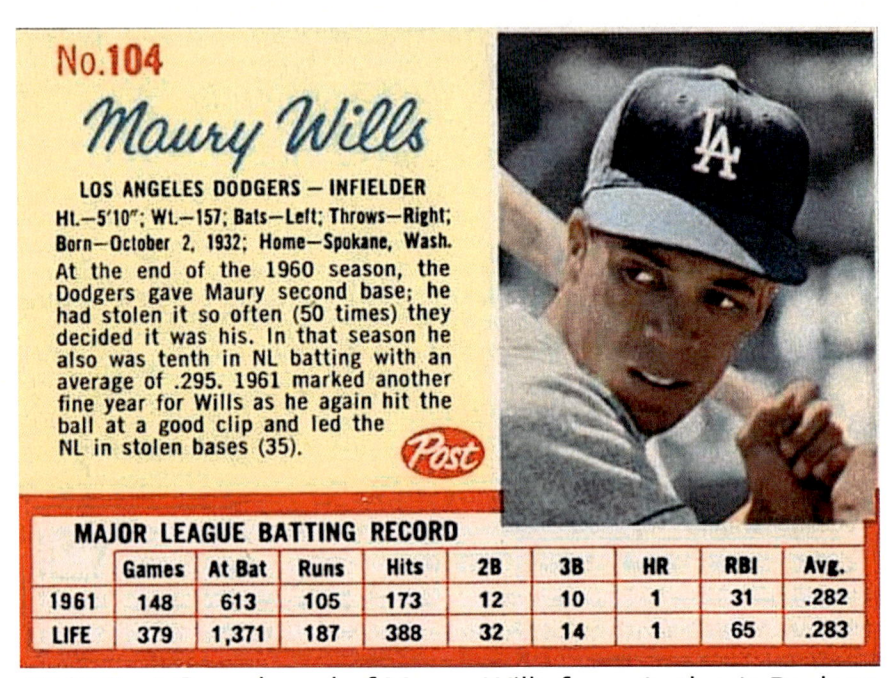

1961 Post Cereal card of Maury Wills from Author's Dodger Museum Collection

This relentless dedication converged with a seismic shift in baseball when the Brooklyn Dodgers, after years of frustration over a new stadium, packed their bags for the burgeoning, sun-drenched sprawl of Los Angeles in 1958. The move from the gritty, tradition-steeped Flatbush neighborhood to the gleaming, future-oriented West Coast demanded a new identity for the venerable franchise. The familiar roar of the Brooklyn faithful was replaced by the unfamiliar echoes of the vast Los Angeles Memorial Coliseum, requiring a fresh brand of baseball to resonate with a city enthusiastically embracing change. When Maury Wills finally stepped onto a major league field for the Los Angeles Dodgers on June 6, 1959, at the relatively late age of 26, it was not merely a personal triumph. He was stepping into the enormous shadow cast by Harold "Pee Wee" Reese, the beloved "Boys of Summer" captain and the symbolic heart and soul of the Brooklyn Dodgers for nearly two decades, who had retired just before the team's inaugural LA season. This context made Wills's path to the starting shortstop job even more challenging; he wasn't just competing for a spot, but tasked with helping a new city connect with a team that felt alien to some, all while trying to live up to the immense legacy of a man synonymous with Dodger baseball. Nevertheless, it became clear that this electrifying, unpredictable talent, forged in the crucible of his early life and a grueling minor league apprenticeship, was precisely what the nascent West Coast franchise needed. Wills's dynamic, game-changing speed was not just a tactic but a jolt of energy, a symbol of the exciting, fast-paced future the Los Angeles Dodgers were about to embody, moving beyond the power game of the past. This hard-won opportunity immediately manifested itself in his revolutionary approach to stolen bases. In the early 1960s, baseball had largely abandoned the stolen base as a primary offensive weapon, with the game increasingly dominated by the long ball and the "three true outcomes."

ALLEN SCHERY

At times it seemed Maury Wills "floated" through the air!

Yet, Wills, with his meticulous study of pitchers' deliveries, pickoff moves, and catchers' arms, combined with his explosive first step and uncanny instincts for timing, saw a significant opening. He wasn't necessarily the fastest man in baseball, but he was arguably the most innovative, intelligent, and determined base runner, almost single-handedly bringing the stolen base back into vogue. He transformed it from an occasional tactic into a formidable offensive strategy, proving that a team didn't need to rely solely on home runs to score; they could consistently manufacture runs through speed, aggressive baserunning, and by putting constant pressure on the defense. His 1962 MVP season was the ultimate testament to this philosophy, as he shattered Ty Cobb's long-standing modern-era record of 96 stolen bases, swiping an astonishing 104 bags. This was not just a number; it was a cultural phenomenon. The "Go! Go! Go!" chant from the Dodger Stadium crowd became iconic, signaling a dramatic shift in how fans perceived the game and what defined exciting baseball. His success was so profound that in 1962 he stole more bases than any single team in Major League Baseball (the Washington Senators led the American League with 99 steals, and the Dodgers themselves, excluding Wills, stole only 47). Even when Wills didn't steal, his mere presence on base created immense pressure on opposing pitchers and catchers, forcing them to constantly consider him, altering their focus and potentially leading to mistakes or poor pitch execution. Opposing managers would resort to desperate, even absurd measures, like San Francisco Giants manager Alvin Dark infamously ordering the base paths watered down at Candlestick Park to try and slow Wills down—a testament to the fear and disruption he instilled. For the Los Angeles Dodgers, Wills's speed perfectly complemented their dominant pitching staff of Sandy Koufax and Don Drysdale, defining the "pitching, defense, and speed" philosophy that became the hallmark of the wildly successful Dodger teams of the 1960s. These teams won three World Series titles (1959, 1963, 1965) with Wills as their catalyst and captain (1963-1966). Beyond his offense, Wills was also a two-time Gold Glove winner (1961, 1962), demonstrating his all-around value at a crucial defensive position. His 14-year career would see him play for the Dodgers across two distinct stints, separated by brief, yet impactful, tenures with the Pittsburgh Pirates and Montreal Expos. After the Dodgers' disappointing loss in the 1966 World Series, the team embarked on a grueling postseason exhibition tour of Japan. Wills, who had battled persistent knee injuries throughout the latter part of the 1966 season and felt unable to perform, made the decision to leave the Japan tour midway through, departing on October 27, 1966, after only four games, to return home for treatment. However, instead of heading directly back to Los Angeles for rehabilitation, Wills made an unauthorized detour to Hawaii, where he publicly performed his banjo in various shows, notably with entertainers like Sammy Davis Jr. and Don Ho. This public display of leisure and entertainment, occurring while the team was still on its grueling tour and while Wills was ostensibly sidelined for a serious injury, deeply displeased

Dodgers owner Walter O'Malley, who viewed it as a serious breach of expected conduct. It's important to note that Wills' departure from the tour and his Hawaii stop occurred before Sandy Koufax's highly anticipated retirement announcement on November 18, 1966, though Koufax had reportedly made his decision well before the season's end. As Wills himself recounted about O'Malley's reaction, "So, I got my own ticket and went home. The late Walter O'Malley didn't like it, and he got rid of me—they traded me to the Pirates. I cried for a week when I heard about it."

On December 1, 1966, just weeks after the Japan tour and Koufax's announcement, the Dodgers traded Wills to the Pittsburgh Pirates in exchange for third baseman Bob Bailey and shortstop Gene Michael. Wills spent the 1967 and 1968 seasons with the Pirates, primarily playing shortstop, but also seeing time at third base. While O'Malley was clearly unhappy with Wills' action in Japan and the highly publicized "Banjo Incident" in Hawaii, the trade's rationale, from the club's perspective, was part of a broader strategy to introduce younger talent. Wills, then 34 years old and having played the last seven seasons with the club, represented a veteran presence in a team looking toward future turnover. Dodgers management, including O'Malley and General Manager Emil "Buzzie" Bavasi, often expressed the need to get younger and prepare for the next generation of players following the end of the 1960s dynasty Notably, his relationship with the Dodgers eventually mended, as evidenced by his return to the team in 1969. Upon Maury's return, O'Malley himself extended a personal welcome, famously writing a note to him in the Dodgers clubhouse: "Welcome back, Maury."

However, his time in Pittsburgh was also short-lived. In the 1969 Expansion Draft, the Pirates left Wills unprotected, and the newly formed Montreal Expos selected him as their 21st pick. Wills initially expressed reluctance to play for an expansion team, even hinting at retirement if drafted by one, and his brief tenure in Montreal was marked by a contract holdout, indifferent play where he struggled at the plate (batting around .222), and even a brief "retirement" before he was persuaded to return. Seeing an opportunity to bring back a fan favorite and a player who perfectly embodied their "pitching, defense, and speed" philosophy, the Dodgers re-acquired Maury Wills. On June 11, 1969, Los Angeles traded outfielder Ron Fairly and infielder Paul Popovich to the Expos for Wills and outfielder Manny Mota. This move proved to be a stroke of genius, as Mota became a highly valuable pinch-hitter for the Dodgers, and Wills, back in familiar surroundings, regained his form, finishing his career with the team that had given him his major league start, retiring in 1972 with 2,134 hits, 586 stolen bases (putting him 20th all-time), 1,067 runs scored, and a career .281 batting average. His daring play and innovative baserunning influenced future legends like Lou Brock and Rickey Henderson, fundamentally altering their approach to the game and proving that speed was a legitimate and powerful weapon, thus opening the door for a renewed emphasis on athleticism and baserunning throughout the sport. However, Maury Wills's story extends far beyond the diamond. After his illustrious playing career, he embarked on a less successful managerial career, most notably with the Seattle Mariners in 1980-81. His tenure there was marred by poor on-field performance (a 26-56 record in 1980 and 24-56 in 1981, leading to his dismissal), and a highly publicized controversial suspension for tampering with the batter's box by widening it by several inches, a desperate attempt to give his struggling hitters an advantage. More significantly, his post-playing years were marked by a severe struggle with drug and alcohol addiction, a battle he courageously fought and ultimately overcame with the unwavering support of friends and former teammates, particularly Peter O'Malley, the then-Dodgers owner, who paid for his treatment and gave him a chance to return to the organization. His remarkable candidness about his addiction and subsequent sobriety became a powerful testament to his resilience, transforming him into a vocal advocate for recovery. He returned to baseball as a special instructor, particularly for baserunning, sharing the wisdom gained from his groundbreaking career. He often worked with young players for the Dodgers and other organizations, including a long and affectionate association with the independent league Fargo-Moorhead RedHawks as a coach and broadcaster. His journey of overcoming adversity became as much a part of his legacy as his stolen base records. Despite his undeniable impact on the game's strategy, his record-breaking 1962 season, and his impressive statistical achievements, Wills faced a perplexing uphill battle for election to the National Baseball Hall of Fame. He consistently fell short of the required votes by the Baseball Writers' Association of America and later by various Veterans Committees, a fact that often frustrated those who witnessed his electrifying career and understood his profound influence on how baseball was played. Many argued that the Hall's traditional focus on power numbers and pitching wins overlooked the significant strategic shift he initiated. . Nevertheless, his enduring presence as a Dodger ambassador, his distinctive banjo playing (which he famously performed on television, in Las Vegas clubs, and at Dodger fan events), and his role as a mentor to players and an inspiration to those battling addiction cemented his place not just as a baseball icon, but as a complex and ultimately triumphant figure whose impact resonated far beyond the confines of a baseball field until his passing in 2022 at the age of 89. Maury added unique color for the first-generation Los Angeles Dodger fans. There was always the joke about the "Maury Wills Triple". It started with a bunt or a walk, stealing second and third base followed and scoring on a sacrifice fly soon followed. Beyond that was the endless "charge" cry let out as soon as Maury got on base as if the cavalry just arrived! The fans loved it.

maury wills

LOS ANGELES DODGERS
SHORTSTOP

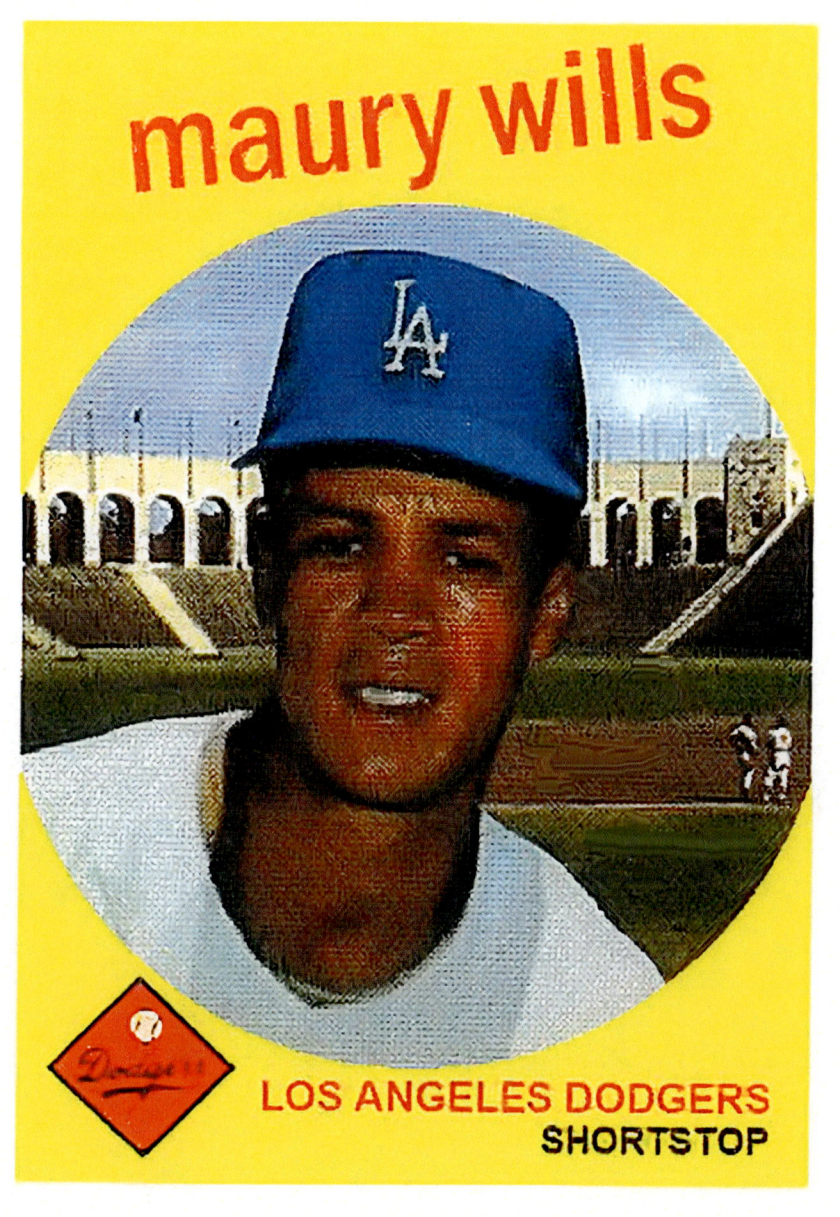

Maury Wills began his base stealing barrage at the Coliseum.

ALLEN SCHERY

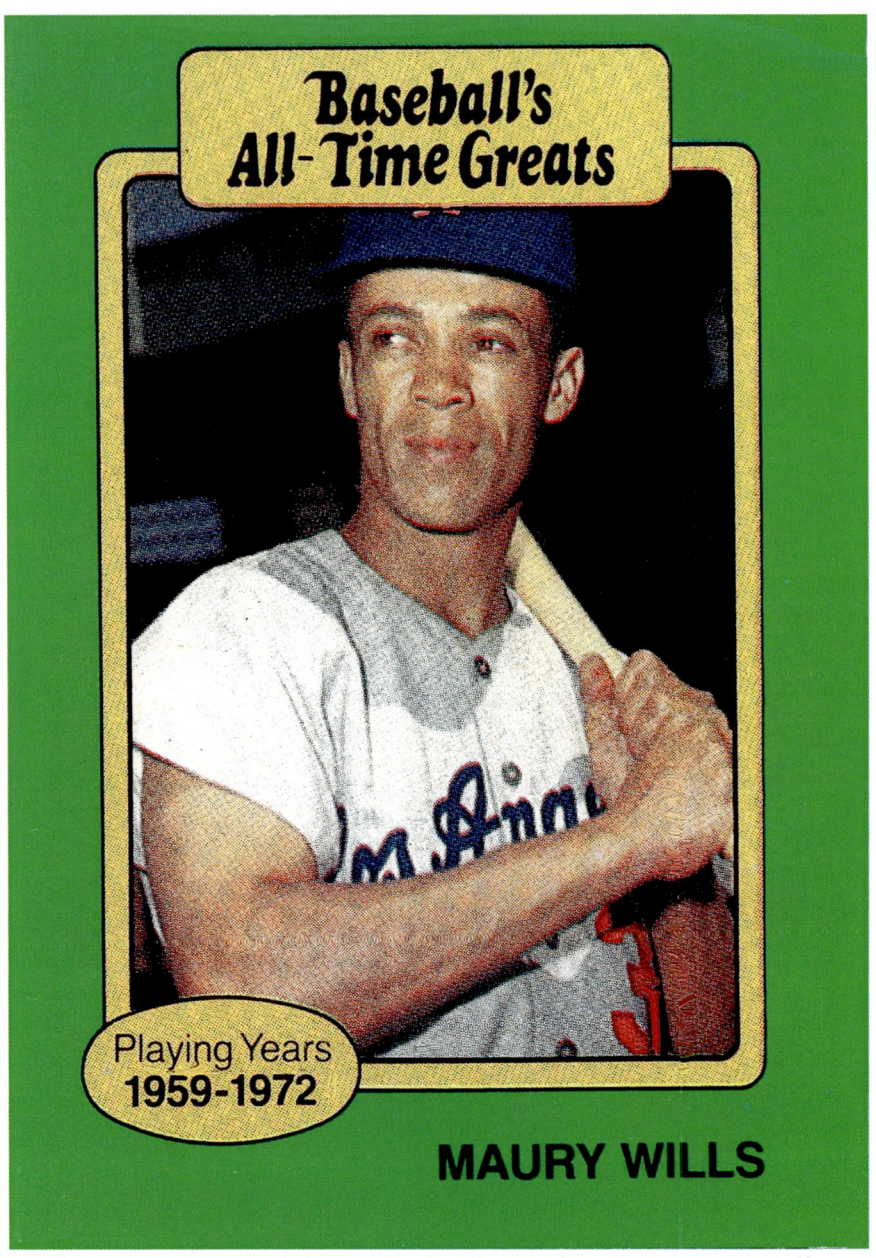

Hygrade Wills card from Author's Dodger Museum Collection.

Chapter Five

The Cinderella Story: How the '59 Pennant Was Won.

The 1959 Los Angeles Dodgers, just their second season in the sprawling, car-centric metropolis, were not supposed to be contenders. Fresh off a disappointing seventh-place finish in their inaugural National League campaign at the cavernous Los Angeles Memorial Coliseum, a temporary home with arguably the most unconventional dimensions in Major League Baseball history, expectations were, at best, modest. Many preseason prognosticators had pegged them for another bottom-half finish, questioning whether the Brooklyn magic could truly translate to the West Coast. Yet, what unfolded over the course of that summer was a captivating narrative of resilience, unexpected brilliance, and a collective will to win that culminated in one of baseball's most improbable Cinderella stories. The '59 pennant wasn't merely won; it was seized through a dramatic season-long struggle that captivated a new fan base and solidified the Dodgers' place in the heart of Hollywood.

1958 Bell Brand Potato Chips Team Set from Author's Dodger Museum Collection.

    The season began with an air of uncertainty. The previous year had been a rude awakening for a franchise accustomed to Brooklyn glory. Now, playing in a football stadium ill-suited for baseball, with a short-left field and a massive expanse in right, the team needed to adapt, and quickly. Manager Walter Alston, a man of quiet determination and unwavering stoicism, faced the daunting task of molding a cohesive unit from a mix of seasoned veterans, some still adjusting to life outside Brooklyn's familiar confines, and unproven youngsters. His calm demeanor and consistent approach, often characterized by his famous one-year contracts that kept him perpetually proving himself, would prove invaluable in navigating the pressures of a pennant race, instilling a quiet confidence that permeated the clubhouse.

While the Dodgers lacked a single, overpowering superstar in 1959, their strength lay in their pitching, particularly their formidable starting rotation. Don Drysdale, then a lanky 22-year-old fireballer, emerged as the ace. He led the pitching staff with an impressive 17 wins against 13 losses, showcasing his intimidating presence on the mound and his ability to work out of jams. His fastball, often described as "unhittable," and his sharp curveball were a potent combination that kept opposing hitters off balance. Complementing Drysdale were the steady and reliable Johnny Podres, who contributed 14 wins with a respectable 3.75 ERA. The crafty left-hander Sandy Koufax, still honing his legendary talent, showed flashes of brilliance with 8 wins, but his control was still a work in progress, evidenced by his league-leading 98 walks. The bullpen, initially a question mark, solidified around the emergence of Larry Sherry. Sherry, a young right-hander who had made only a handful of appearances in 1958, truly broke out in 1959, becoming a crucial late-inning reliever with a deceptive delivery and nerves of steel. His ability to pitch in high-leverage situations would prove pivotal as the season wore on.

Offensively, the Dodgers were a scrappy bunch, not reliant on the long ball but instead focusing on timely hitting, smart base running, and a tenacious approach at the plate. Wally Moon, acquired in an off-season trade from the St. Louis Cardinals for Gino Cimoli, famously adapted his swing to the Coliseum's unique dimensions. His distinctive high, arcing "Moon Shots" over the short left-field screen became an immediate fan favorite and an offensive catalyst tailored perfectly to the temporary ballpark. He led the team in home runs with 19 and RBIs with 74, while hitting for a .302 average. His ability to hit these strategic line drives over the short porch in the Coliseum proved invaluable in manufacturing runs.

Charlie Neal, the second baseman, enjoyed a breakout season, providing both power and speed, hitting 19 home runs and driving in 83 runs. His solid defense up the middle was also a significant asset, and he finished the season with a .287 batting average.

Norm Larker, a left-handed hitting first baseman and occasional outfielder, was a quiet but consistent offensive force for the 1959 Dodgers. In his sophomore season, Larker raised his batting average to a solid .289 across 108 games. He contributed 8 home runs and 49 RBIs, providing dependable offense from the cleanup or middle of the order. He split his time, starting 55 games at first base and 30 in the outfield,

Charlie Neal 1959 Morrell Meats Card from Author's Dodger Museum Collection.

showcasing his versatility. While Gil Hodges remained the veteran presence at first base and provided crucial leadership, Larker's consistent bat and solid defense allowed him to play a significant role, particularly as Hodges dealt with nagging injuries throughout the season.

Larker's plate discipline was also notable, with his ability to make contact and avoid strikeouts. His contributions were vital in maintaining offensive pressure throughout the long season, setting the table for and driving in runs. He continued this clutch hitting into the postseason, notably collecting five hits in eight at-bats with three RBIs during the two-game playoff sweep against the Braves.

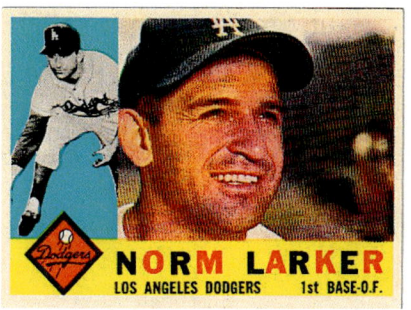

Norm Larker 1960 Topps Card # 394 from Author's Dodger Museum Collection.

One of the most significant factors in the Dodgers' resurgence was the infusion of fresh talent and the unexpected rise of unheralded players, contributing to the team's overall depth and versatility. Maury Wills, a name that would become synonymous with base-stealing dominance in the coming years, made his major league debut in 1959. Though he only played 83 games, his electrifying speed and aggressive base-running immediately injected a new dynamic into the Dodgers' offense. While his 7 stolen bases in 1959 weren't indicative of his future prowess, his mere presence on base created havoc for opposing pitchers and catchers, forcing them to consider the run game in every situation. Wills' arrival marked the beginning of a shift in the Dodgers' offensive philosophy, leaning into speed and small ball.

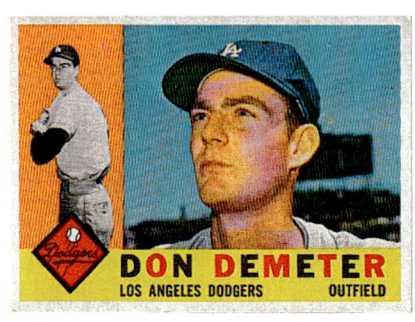

Another critical newcomer was Don Demeter, who contributed 18 home runs and 70 RBIs, providing much-needed power from the outfield. Veteran catcher John Roseboro took over the lion's share of catching duties, displaying strong defensive skills and a burgeoning bat, hitting .291 with 5 home runs and 43 RBIs. Frank Howard, a towering slugger who would go on to have a prolific career, also made his debut in 1959, though his full impact would be felt in later seasons. The contributions of these newer players, seamlessly integrating with the established veterans, created a deep and versatile roster. Jim Gilliam, a veteran who seamlessly transitioned to various positions, including third base, provided invaluable versatility and a knack for getting on base, drawing a team-leading 96 walks. His steady presence and ability to bat left-handed against right-handed pitching made him an indispensable part of Alston's strategic lineup.

Don Demeter 1960 Topps Card # 294 from Author's Dodger Museum Collection.

While the team on the field battled for the pennant, team owner Walter O'Malley remained actively engaged in shaping the franchise's future in Los Angeles. As President of the Dodgers, O'Malley's focus in 1959 extended beyond the current season's performance. He continued to manage the team's business operations, overseeing everything from radio and television contracts to promotions, and ensuring the development of the Vero Beach spring training facility, Dodgertown, which had quickly become a crucial part of the organization's player development and scouting efforts. Crucially, 1959 was a pivotal year for O'Malley's long-term vision for the Dodgers' permanent home. Despite facing ongoing legal hurdles and lawsuits that sought to block the city's contract with the Dodgers, delaying construction, O'Malley was determined to build a state-of-the-art ballpark. He tirelessly worked to secure the necessary funding and overcome political opposition, frequently dealing with the media and public opinion. On September 17, 1959, he proudly participated in the groundbreaking ceremonies for the privately built Dodger Stadium in Chavez Ravine, alongside civic officials and construction chiefs. This event, just weeks before the dramatic pennant clincher, signaled O'Malley's unwavering commitment to creating a lasting legacy for the Dodgers in Los Angeles, even as the team played its games in the temporary, yet record-setting, Coliseum. His strategic foresight and unwavering dedication to building a permanent home undoubtedly contributed to stability and burgeoning confidence within the organization, assuring fans that the team was here to stay.

Amidst the early uncertainties and the developing team identity, a truly special moment transcended the daily grind of the baseball season. On May 7, 1959, the Dodgers hosted "Roy Campanella Night" at the Coliseum. It was an exhibition game against their old rivals, the New York Yankees, organized specifically to help defray the considerable medical expenses of their beloved former catcher, who had been paralyzed in a devastating car accident in January 1958. That night, an astonishing 93,103 fans packed the Coliseum, setting a new world record for the largest crowd ever to attend a baseball game. The immense turnout was a testament to Campanella's enduring popularity and the new city's embrace of its adopted team, defying skepticism about whether Los Angeles could truly support a Major League Baseball franchise on such a scale. During an emotional ceremony between the fifth and sixth innings, the stadium lights were dimmed, and fans were asked to light matches or lighters, creating a breathtaking, twinkling panorama of devotion across the vast Coliseum.

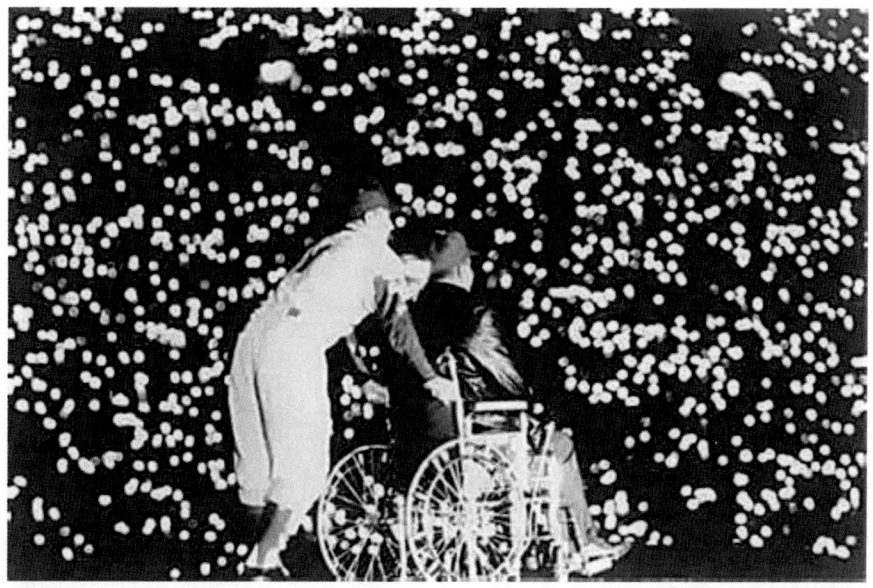

On May 7, 1959, the Dodgers hosted "Roy Campanella Night" at the Coliseum.

The sight was electrifying, a sea of flickering lights honoring a hero. In a moment that resonated deeply with both Brooklyn faithful and new Angelenos, Pee Wee Reese, Campanella's longtime teammate and friend, wheeled the paralyzed catcher onto the field. The roar of the crowd was deafening, a profound outpouring of love and respect for Campanella, who, despite his physical limitations, remained inextricably linked to the Dodgers' heart and soul. This event, so early in the season, served as a powerful reminder of the team's rich history and its ability to unite people through shared emotional experiences.

ALLEN SCHERY

Don Drysdale at the Coliseum. At 6' 6" he was an intimidating figure.

It solidified the bond between the franchise and its burgeoning Los Angeles fanbase, offering a glimpse of the powerful emotional connection that would soon define Dodgers baseball in Southern California. The game itself, an exhibition won by the Yankees 6-2, was almost secondary to the profound tribute paid to Campy.

"A lot of people didn't know the man (O'Malley) for what he was," said Campanella to the Los Angeles Times the day O'Malley passed in 1979. "He stood by me every minute after my accident, helping me to see my way through. No one knows that after that wonderful night he had for me in the Coliseum when 93,000 showed up, he gave me a check for $50,000. And he continued my salary, which was more than $50,000 a year, for years after that. He was a great pioneer in integrating baseball."

League Leaders and Individual Excellence

While no single Dodger dominated the league leaderboards in multiple categories, the team's success was built on a collective effort with several players performing at an All-Star level and contributing significantly to the team's overall statistics.

- Don Drysdale: As mentioned, Drysdale's 17 wins were a team high and among the best in the league. His 175 strikeouts also placed him among the National League's top pitchers.

- Wally Moon: His .302 batting average was among the team's best, and his 19 home runs and 74 RBIs were crucial offensive production, making him a consistent threat at the plate, especially with his unique "Moon Shot" ability.
- Charlie Neal: His 19 home runs and 83 RBIs showcased his offensive breakout, establishing him as a potent bat in the middle of the lineup and providing unexpected power from a middle infielder.
- Johnny Podres: His 14 wins provided a solid number two starter behind Drysdale, often stepping up with key performances when the team needed them most.
- Norm Larker: His consistent .289 batting average and ability to get on base provided essential support in the Dodgers' lineup, demonstrating reliable contact hitting.
- Maury Wills: While not a league leader in 1959, his emergence signaled a future shift in the game, and his early impact on the base paths with his speed was undeniable, laying the groundwork for his legendary stolen base records to come.
- Larry Sherry: Though his win-loss record (7-2) wasn't eye-popping, his crucial 7 saves and stifling bullpen performances were invaluable and often unquantifiable by traditional stats, solidifying his role as the team's most trusted late-inning reliever.
- Jim Gilliam: His 96 walks were a testament to his plate discipline, and his versatile defense made him an unsung hero.

1958 Hires Root Beer Dodgers Team Set from Author's Dodger Museum Collection.

    The Dodgers, like any team, faced their share of adversity. After a strong start, they hit a mid-season slump, falling behind the Milwaukee Braves and the San Francisco Giants in the standings. Injuries played a role, with key players missing time, and the relentless pressure of a pennant race began to take its toll. The vastness of the Coliseum, while a draw for fans, also presented unique challenges for fielders, particularly in the immense outfield, and the team had to adjust its defensive strategies and positioning to minimize extra-base hits. However, the Dodgers never truly gave up. Alston's calm demeanor and unwavering belief in his players kept the team grounded, preventing panic from setting in. The veterans, including Pee Wee Reese, who, though no longer an active player after retiring in 1958, remained a revered figure and provided invaluable leadership and a link to the team's Brooklyn past as a coach, and Gil Hodges, the dependable first baseman and a powerful presence at the plate, helped maintain a positive clubhouse atmosphere and offered veteran guidance to the younger players. The team displayed a remarkable ability to bounce back from losses, often winning crucial games immediately after a disappointing defeat. Their home record at the Coliseum, where they thrived on the energy of the large crowds that often exceeded 60,000, was a significant factor in their ability to stay in the race, giving them a distinct home-field advantage. The Dodgers, in fact, set an all-time Major League Baseball attendance record in 1959, drawing over 2.2 million fans, a testament to the city's immediate embrace and the excitement the team generated. The "pitching, defense, and speed" philosophy, which would become a hallmark of the Alston Dodgers, was homed in the crucible of the Coliseum, perfectly suited to manufacturing runs and grinding out close victories.

The 1959 National League pennant race became an instant classic, a nail-biting, three-way struggle involving the Dodgers, the Milwaukee Braves, and the San Francisco Giants. As September arrived, the lead changed hands almost daily, with each team exchanging blows in a relentless battle for supremacy. Every game felt like a playoff game, with the pressure mounting on all three contenders, captivating baseball fans across the country. This race was made all the more compelling by the burgeoning "California rivalry" between the Dodgers and the Giants, two former New York titans now battling for supremacy on the West Coast. The Dodgers, fueled by a late-season surge, caught fire in the final weeks, showing incredible resolve. Key victories against direct rivals proved decisive, particularly crucial series against the Giants and Braves that often took on the intensity of postseason matchups. The Coliseum, with its massive crowds, became a cauldron of excitement, as fans eagerly followed every pitch and every play. The home stand that opened the final week of the season was particularly crucial, as the Dodgers swept a series that propelled them into a tie for first place. On the final day of the regular season, the drama reached its peak. The Dodgers faced the Chicago Cubs, while the Braves played the San Francisco Giants. The Dodgers, needing a win to secure at least a tie, defeated the Cubs 7-4. However, the Braves also won their game, leading to a tie for first place with identical records of 86 wins and 68 losses for both the Dodgers and the Braves. The San Francisco Giants finished just two games back, completing one of the closest three-team races in National League history.

 The tie necessitated a best-of-three playoff series to determine the National League pennant winner. This was uncharted territory for the new Los Angeles Dodgers, and the city was abuzz with anticipation, desperate for their first championship. The series would begin in Milwaukee. Game 1 (Milwaukee, September 28th): The Dodgers sent Don Drysdale to the mound against the Braves' Lew Burdette. It was a classic pitching duel, a tense, low-scoring affair. The Dodgers scratched out a crucial 3-2 victory in 10 innings, with the winning run coming on an error, giving them an early advantage. Game 2 (Los Angeles, September 29th): The series shifted to the Los Angeles Memorial Coliseum, where an astounding 92,000+ fans packed the stands, setting a new record for a non-World Series baseball game. The atmosphere was electric. Johnny Podres started for the Dodgers against Bob Rush. The game was another tense, low-scoring affair. The Dodgers eventually prevailed with a 6-5 victory in 12 innings, sealing the National League pennant in dramatic fashion. The winning run scored on a sacrifice fly by Gil Hodges, driving in Wally Moon, sending the Coliseum crowd into an absolute frenzy that seemed to shake the very foundations of the immense stadium. The scene at the Coliseum after the final out was pure pandemonium. Thousands of fans, unable to contain their excitement, streamed onto the field, engulfing their heroes in a joyous celebration. Players were mobbed, hoisted onto shoulders, and cheered as the reality of their improbable pennant sunk in. It was a powerful visual representation of the bridge between Brooklyn's past and Los Angeles's hopeful future, a testament to the fact that the "Dodger spirit" had successfully migrated west. This hard-fought National League championship, achieved against all odds in just their second year in Los Angeles, was a profound statement.

The Coliseum was the Dodgers Los Angeles home from 1958-1961.

It proved that this new iteration of the Dodgers, playing in their unconventional home, was truly a force to be reckoned with. The Cinderella story had delivered them to the precipice of ultimate glory, as the '59 Dodgers prepared to face their next challenge: the Chicago White Sox in the World Series, a contest they would ultimately win in six games, completing their improbable championship season.

ALLEN SCHERY

Era Topps Cards from Author's Dodger Museum Collection.

Chapter Six

A World Series for a New Home: Triumph in the City of Angels featuring Fairfax High School Heroes Larry Sherry and Chuck Essegian.

The Dodgers' controversial relocation to Los Angeles had been a whirlwind of change, filled with initial skepticism and the awkward, often challenging, adaptation to the sprawling Los Angeles Memorial Coliseum. While the previous chapters have detailed the dramatic 1959 regular season and the grueling National League Playoff Series, this chapter unveils the ultimate climax: the World Series. It was here, on baseball's grandest stage, that the Dodgers would not only battle for a championship but also for the very soul of their new identity in Southern California. This series was more than a mere sporting event; it was a defining cultural moment, a chance for Los Angeles to unequivocally embrace its newfound major league status and for the Dodgers to forge an unbreakable bond with their burgeoning fanbase. Their unexpected journey, a true Cinderella story that had captivated the city from the first pitch, culminated in a triumph forged by a resilient team and, unexpectedly, by two local heroes from Fairfax High School, Larry Sherry and Chuck Essegian, whose clutch performances would forever link this championship to the very fabric of Los Angeles.

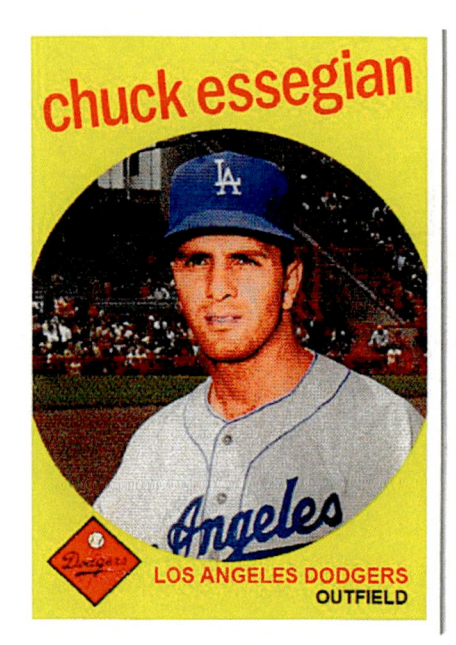

New Home, New Stars Fairfax High School stars lead the way to First Championship Team from Author's Dodger Museum Collection.

Carrying the emotional high of their hard-fought three-game playoff victory over the Milwaukee Braves, the

Dodgers arrived at the World Series with hard-earned momentum. That brutal playoff series had forged a cohesive and resilient unit, a band of brothers ready to face the American League's best: the Chicago White Sox. This was Chicago's first World Series appearance since the infamous 1919 "Black Sox" scandal, adding another layer of historical weight to the matchup for the Windy City. Managed by the astute Al Lopez, the White Sox epitomized "small ball"—a team built on blinding speed, stellar pitching, and airtight defense, earning them the nickname "The Go-Go White Sox." Their lineup featured gritty MVP second baseman Nellie Fox, a master of contact hitting and defensive wizardry, and the electrifying shortstop Luis Aparicio, whose blazing speed terrorized basepaths and whose glove seemed to vacuum up anything hit his way. Their formidable pitching staff was led by the intimidating veteran ace Early Wynn, a Cy Young Award winner known for his fierce competitiveness and willingness to pitch inside, and the reliable Bob Shaw. Pre-series analysis by the media often heavily favored Chicago, highlighting the clash of styles and questioning how the Coliseum-adapted Dodgers, with their penchant for "Moon Shots," would fare in a traditional, pitcher-friendly ballpark like Comiskey Park. Conversely, there was also speculation on how Chicago's speed game, reliant on gaps and extra bases, would translate to the Coliseum's cavernous outfield, which could swallow many potential hits.

Roger Craig, Don Drysdale, Sandy Koufax and Johnny Podres led the pitching staff during Coliseum Era.

The series opened on October 1, 1959, at Comiskey Park, before a jubilant crowd of 48,013 passionate fans, and the White Sox immediately delivered a stunning blow in Game 1. Before their roaring home crowd, Chicago exploded, putting up seven runs in a decisive third inning alone. This massive rally was highlighted by Nellie Fox's bases-clearing triple that emptied the bases and Ted Kluszewski's two-run single, sending a clear message of their offensive prowess. Kluszewski, who had shed his sleeves to famously display his muscular arms, followed up with a towering two-run homer in the fourth, seemingly setting an ominous tone for his impressive series performance. Indeed, Kluszewski would be an offensive force throughout the series, finishing with a remarkable .391 batting average, three home runs, and eight RBIs, proving to be a constant thorn in the Dodgers' side despite their eventual triumph. Early Wynn, living up to his intimidating reputation, masterfully controlled the Dodgers' lineup with his cunning pitches and unwavering composure, allowing just seven hits for a complete-game shutout. Dodgers' starter Roger Craig, a young right-hander, was knocked out early, struggling to find his rhythm and command against the aggressive White Sox hitters. The final score, an 11-0 rout, was a demoralizing start for Los Angeles, instantly deflating the initial wave of West Coast optimism and leaving many wondering if the Cinderella story had finally hit midnight. As usually happens in such cases the game one blowout never saw repeating again. Thankfully it was a red herring but many of the other games were close pitcher duels. This was all new fare for the Los Angeles Dodger fans as it was their first foray into the experience World Series games.

Game 1 was a blowout. 1960 Topps Card is from Author's Dodger Museum Collection.

Facing a daunting 0-1 deficit and the psychological weight of such a dominant Game 1 loss, the Dodgers needed an immediate response in Game 2, played on October 2 at Comiskey Park before a crowd of 47,368. Don Drysdale, their imposing ace, took the mound for Los Angeles against Bob Shaw. The White Sox initially continued their momentum, taking an early 2-0 lead, threatening to push the Dodgers to the brink. However, the Dodgers, known for their scrappy resilience, chipped away. Wally Moon, ever the clutch hitter, launched a crucial solo home run in the fifth inning, a traditional shot that showcased his ability to hit effectively even outside the Coliseum's quirks. The pivotal turning point arrived in the seventh when Norm Larker's RBI single tied the game, demonstrating the team's ability to manufacture runs. Carl Furillo's sacrifice fly in the eighth then gave the Dodgers their first lead of the series, a hard-earned advantage.

Critically, after Drysdale struggled early but settled into a more effective groove, Manager Walter Alston made a decision that would define the series: he boldly summoned Larry Sherry from the bullpen in the sixth inning with runners on base and the game hanging precariously in the balance. Sherry, a quiet, unassuming right-hander, calmly and methodically worked out of the jam, showcasing remarkable composure under immense pressure.

His 2.2 innings of brilliant shutout relief, allowing only one hit, not only earned him the win but also signaled the unexpected emergence of a true postseason hero. Alston's unconventional, yet prescient, reliance on Sherry would become a hallmark of his shrewd managerial style throughout the series, demonstrating his willingness to deviate from traditional roles to secure victory.

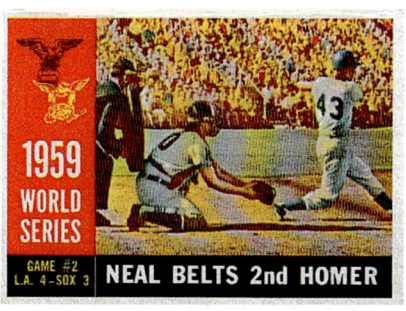

1960 Topps Game Two World Series Card from Author's Dodger Museum Collection.

The series then moved to Los Angeles for Game 3 on October 4, ushering in an unprecedented spectacle at the Los Angeles Memorial Coliseum. In Game 5 92,706 fans packed the temporary ballpark, smashing the attendance record set just five years earlier in the 1954 World Series. The stadium, despite its odd configuration, hummed with an electric atmosphere, a palpable testament to LA's passionate embrace of its new team. The sheer size of the Coliseum outfield, with its sprawling power alleys, also inadvertently helped neutralize the White Sox's speed game, turning many of their potential extra-base hits into singles or outs, thus playing into the Dodgers' hands. Johnny Podres, the hero of the 1955

World Series with Brooklyn, took the mound for the Dodgers against Dick Donovan.

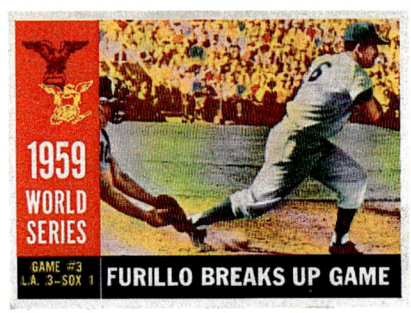

Carl Furillo knocked in first two runs of Game Three of 1959 World Series.

Podres delivered a masterful complete-game performance, expertly navigating the White Sox's speed and neutralizing their small-ball tactics with pinpoint control and clever pitch selection. While the Dodgers scored two runs in the third inning, the true moment of local fanfare came in the seventh: Chuck Essegian, a previously unheralded reserve outfielder and pinch-hitter extraordinaire, stepped to the plate and, in a moment of pure Hollywood drama, launched a dramatic solo home run off Donovan, a towering shot over the left field screen. This unexpected blast extended the Dodgers' lead to 3-1, and the massive crowd erupted into a deafening roar, celebrating a vital insurance run and a truly unexpected local hero.

Confidence surged through the Dodger clubhouse as they headed into Game 4 on October 5, another Coliseum spectacle with 92,650 fans in attendance, demonstrating the sustained fever pitch in Los Angeles. In a bold and surprising move, Walter Alston sent Roger Craig to the mound as the starter against Early Wynn, giving the young right-hander a shot at redemption. The gamble initially backfired, as Craig gave up four runs and was pulled early in the game. However, the Dodgers' bullpen, displaying its newfound depth and resilience, immediately stepped up. Larry Sherry, continuing his incredible postseason run, delivered an exceptional performance in relief, calming the waters and stifling the White Sox offense.

The Dodgers' offense, known for its scrappiness, rallied from behind, sparked by Gil Hodges' two-run double and John Roseboro's RBI single, which helped them claw back to take the lead. Sherry was brought back in to get the final out of the ninth inning,

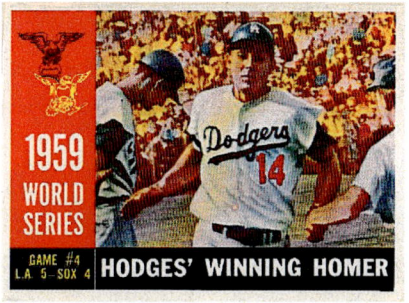

Gil Hodges eighth inning Home Run won Game Four of 1959 World Series/

securing the save and his second victory of the series. But Sherry wasn't the only local hero making noise: Chuck Essegian cemented his status by hitting his second pinch-hit home run of the series, a solo shot off none other than the formidable Early Wynn in the eighth inning. This provided yet another crucial insurance run and marked a truly rare historical feat—the first player ever to hit two pinch-hit home runs in a single World Series, further solidifying the narrative of unlikely heroes.

With a commanding 3-1 series lead, the Dodgers had a golden opportunity to clinch the championship at the Coliseum in Game 5 on October 6. The atmosphere was thick with anticipation, the air practically buzzing with the promise of a long-awaited celebration. In game five a record shattering 92,706 fans attended breaking the record formerly set in 1954. Sandy Koufax, still finding his consistent command but capable of flashes of brilliance, took the mound for the Dodgers against Bob Shaw in what quickly became a classic pitchers' duel. Both aces were brilliant through eight innings, allowing no runs and showcasing their masterful control and strategic pitching. The tension mounted with every pitch, each out drawing the crowd deeper into the gripping drama. Unfortunately for the Dodgers and the eager home crowd, the White Sox finally broke through in the fourth inning when Nellie Fox, a master at getting on base, scored on a double play off the bat of Sherm Lollar, producing the game's only run. The heartbreaking 1-0 loss was a bitter pill to swallow for the jubilant home crowd, forcing the series back to Chicago for Game 6 and delaying the celebration that had seemed so inevitable just hours before. The stage was now set for the decisive Game 6 on October 8, back at Comiskey Park, with the weight of the season resting on every player's shoulders. Johnny Podres, the seasoned veteran who had already proven his World Series mettle, started for the Dodgers against Early Wynn, making his third start of the series. This time, the Dodgers didn't wait to make their mark. Their offense, perhaps fueled by the disappointment of Game 5, exploded for six runs in a pivotal third inning, effectively chasing Wynn from the game early in his own ballpark.

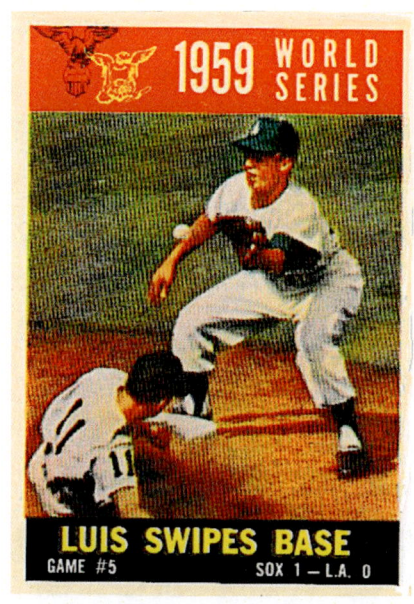

Sandy Koufax lost Game Five 1-0 when a run scored on a Double Play.

The stage was now set for the decisive Game 6 on October 8, back at Comiskey Park, with the weight of the season resting on every player's shoulders. Johnny Podres, the seasoned veteran who had already proven his World Series mettle, started for the Dodgers against Early Wynn, making his third start of the series. This time, the Dodgers didn't wait to make their mark. Their offense, perhaps fueled by the disappointment of Game 5, exploded for six runs in a pivotal third inning, effectively chasing Wynn from the game early in his own ballpark. The rally was highlighted by Wally Moon's crucial two-run single, a bases-loaded walk to Johnny Roseboro, and a relentless parade of hits that put the game firmly in the Dodgers' control. Duke Snider, the beloved "Duke of Flatbush" now adapting to Los Angeles, added a two-run home run in the fourth, extending the lead and making a powerful statement that the Dodgers were not to be denied. With Podres having done his part through 2.1 innings, Manager Walter Alston made the call that would define the series and solidify a legend: Larry Sherry was summoned from the bullpen in the third inning and delivered a performance for the ages. He pitched seven masterful innings of relief, allowing only one unearned run on a single hit while striking out seven White Sox batters. Sherry's calm and dominant presence, with his deceptive sinker and unwavering focus, utterly stifled the White Sox offense, turning the remainder of the game into a tense but ultimately controlled march toward victory. The final outs were a moment of pure euphoria for the Dodgers. The crowd, though predominantly White Sox fans, witnessed history as Los Angeles secured its first World Series championship with a resounding 9-3 victory. The final out brought an outpouring of joy and vindication for a team that had defied expectations and captured the hearts of a new city.

Fairfax High School Stars Chuck Essegian and Larry Sherry.

The 1959 World Series would forever be etched in baseball history, largely due to the improbable rise of Larry Sherry, who was rightfully named the World Series MVP. While a reliable reliever throughout the regular season and NL playoffs, his transformation into a postseason phenomenon was entirely unexpected. Across four appearances, including an unconventional start and three crucial relief outings, Sherry amassed an astonishing 2 wins and 4 saves (by 1959 scoring rules) with a minuscule 0.71 ERA over 12 2/3 dominant innings. His ability to consistently deliver under immense pressure, inducing ground balls with his deceptive sinker and maintaining a quiet composure even in the most high-leverage situations, was utterly pivotal to the Dodgers' success. He single-handedly stabilized the Dodgers' bullpen, allowing Manager Alston greater flexibility and tactical options throughout the series. His MVP award was unprecedented for a relief pitcher at the time, underscoring his truly exceptional and unexpected contribution, turning him from an unassuming local player into a national sensation and the face of the Dodgers' triumph. Adding another layer to the narrative of local triumph from Fairfax High School was Larry's older brother, Norm Sherry, who also hailed from the same prestigious Los Angeles alma mater and served as a catcher for the Dodgers in 1959. While Norm's on-field contributions in the World Series were less dramatic than his brother's, his impact on the future of the Dodgers' pitching staff was immeasurable, arguably laying the groundwork for the team's sustained dominance in the coming decade.

Norm Sherry was responsible for Sandy Koufax' success as he advised him not to pitch so hard.

It was Norm Sherry, a veteran catcher and astute student of the game, who famously worked with the struggling young phenom Sandy Koufax in the 1960 season, helping him overcome his perennial wildness. Norm taught Koufax how to harness his incredible talent, most notably by developing a more effective changeup and emphasizing better command over pure velocity, rather than simply trying to overpower every hitter. This mentorship was a profound turning point in Koufax's career, laying the groundwork for his eventual transformation into one of the greatest pitchers in baseball history, a crucial piece of the Dodgers' coming dynasty. The Sherry brothers, both alumni of Fairfax, thus contributed both to the immediate World Series glory and to the franchise's long-term success, cementing their family's unique place in Dodgers lore.

1959 World Champion Los Angeles Dodgers.

Equally impactful, though in fleeting yet explosive moments, was Chuck Essegian, the quintessential reserve outfielder and pinch-hitter. His preparedness for limited opportunities paid off spectacularly in the World Series, turning him into an unlikely hero. In Game 3, stepping to the plate as a pinch-hitter, he launched a dramatic solo home run off Dick Donovan, providing vital insurance and sending the record Coliseum crowd into a frenzy, a scene that perfectly captured the improbable nature of the Dodgers' run. Just one game later, in Game 4, he remarkably repeated the feat, hitting his second pinch-hit home run of the series, a solo shot off none other than the formidable Early Wynn. This unprecedented accomplishment—two pinch-hit home runs in a single World Series—solidified his place in baseball lore, highlighting his uncanny ability to deliver in the clutch and his calm under pressure. Essegian's story, another "local boy makes good" from Fairfax High School, provided a tangible and inspiring link between the team and its new, rapidly growing fan base in Los Angeles, making the victory feel deeply personal for the community.

The immediate aftermath of the World Series victory was a spectacle of unparalleled civic pride, unification of the city's sprawling locations and widespread jubilation. Los Angeles erupted in celebration, culminating in massive victory parades that drew hundreds of thousands, if not a million, jubilant fans to the streets downtown. These parades were a sea of Dodger blue, with ticker tape falling like snow and deafening cheers for their conquering heroes. It was a moment of collective catharsis and pure joy, as the city embraced its champions and declared its place firmly in the national sports landscape. This 1959 triumph decisively solidified the Dodgers' place in the heart of Los Angeles, definitively proving that the city could, and would, passionately support a major league baseball team, finally putting to rest any lingering skepticism from the controversial move from Brooklyn.

The victory was a powerful declaration: the Dodgers were no longer Brooklyn's team, but unequivocally, Los Angeles's own.

The victory also sparked an explosion of the "Go Dodgers!" phenomenon, leading to a rapid and fervent growth of the fan base that quickly supplanted previous Pacific Coast League loyalties, transforming a city of various sporting interests into a baseball town. More than just a win, the 1959 championship served as a foundational moment for the Dodgers' legendary dynasty of the 1960s. It established a winning culture, characterized by exceptional pitching, stifling defense, and opportunistic baserunning, and provided a clear blueprint for future successes, cementing Walter Alston's quiet, steady leadership as a key factor in building perennial contenders. This victory was instrumental in healing the emotional wounds of the Brooklyn departure, allowing Los Angeles to truly claim the team as its own, integrating it deeply into the city's identity and sports fabric. The unexpected heroism of local figures from Fairfax High School like Larry Sherry, Chuck Essegian, and Norm Sherry. Norm's tutoring of Sandy Koufax assured the arrival of a generational talent that made the triumph feel even more personal, creating a lasting and profound bond between the team and the community it now proudly represented. Sandy Koufax was given the moniker "The Left Arm of God" and is considered by many the greatest left-handed pitcher in Baseball History.

Official 1959 Dodger World Series Championship Pennant.

Conclusion: A New Era Forged in Fire

The 1959 World Series was more than just a championship; it was the defining moment for the Los Angeles Dodgers, marking their successful transition and definitive rise to undisputed prominence in a new era of American baseball. The lasting legacy of this team, its players, and the "Miracle of 1959" stands as a testament to unexpected heroics, strategic brilliance, and the resilient spirit of a franchise finding its new, thriving home. It is a timeless underdog story, where the quiet determination of players like Larry Sherry, the unlikely clutch hitting of Chuck Essegian, and the crucial guidance of Norm Sherry behind the scenes, became etched forever in baseball history, forever remembered for their pivotal contributions to the franchise's first and most symbolic Los Angeles championship.

Chapter Seven
The Hangover Effect: The Challenges of Defending a Title 1960.

The glorious high of the 1959 World Series victory, the Los Angeles Dodgers' first championship since their move west, settled over Southern California like a vibrant, lingering warmth. The city, still buzzing from record crowds at the Coliseum and a parade of unprecedented scale, had unequivocally embraced its new heroes. Yet, beneath this pervasive euphoria, an unforeseen and insidious challenge began to brew—what sport historians might term "the hangover effect." Winning, as it turned out, brought its own unique and often subtle burdens: the immense weight of heightened expectations from a city that had quickly become accustomed to triumph, the pervasive toll of mental and physical fatigue accumulated over an intense, extended season, and the fresh, unsettling reality of transitioning, almost overnight, from the scrappy, underestimated hunter to the relentlessly pursued hunted. The 1960 season would be the immediate and rigorous test, one the team, largely intact from its championship roster, would have to navigate with a fundamentally shifted dynamic, facing opponents now determined to prove themselves against the reigning kings. Adding another layer of intrigue to this complex post-championship landscape was the arrival of Frank Howard. Though he debuted late in 1960, earning Rookie of the Year honors in a spectacular display of raw power, his immediate impact positioned him as a towering symbol of both future hope and the immediate, formidable test for the reigning champions, highlighting the blend of continuity and emergent talent that defined this pivotal year.

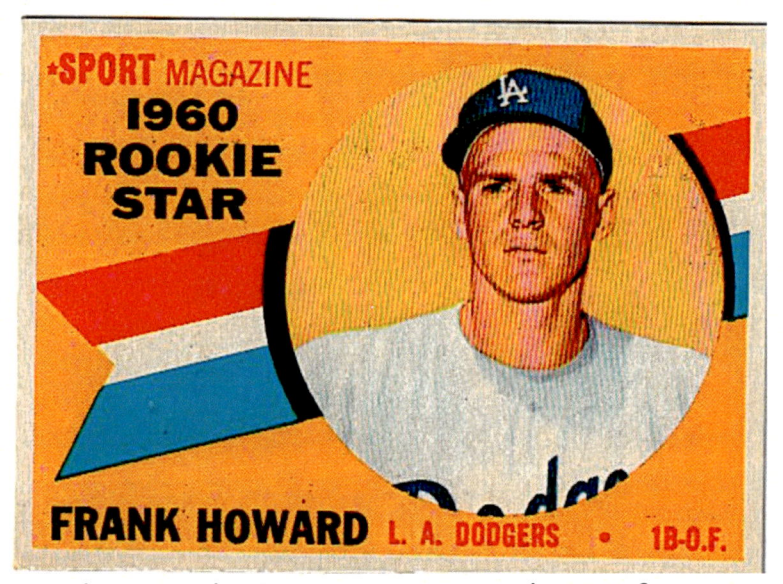

Frank Howard ROY 1960 Topps card # 132 from Authors Dodger Museum Collection.

As the 1960 season dawned, the Dodgers found themselves with an unprecedented target on their backs, visible to every team in the National League. Every opponent now aimed their absolute best, deploying their most aggressive strategies, viewing each matchup as a critical benchmark against the undisputed top dog. The "underdog" mentality that had so powerfully fueled their 1959 triumph, inspiring unexpected heroics and a relentless competitive fire, was replaced by the relentless, often exhausting, pressure of being the team everyone wanted to beat. This wasn't merely about physical exhaustion, though the accumulated minor aches and cumulative wear from a deep playoff run undoubtedly took their toll. It was a deeper, more pervasive psychological drain. Could players maintain the same razor-sharp hunger, the identical singular focus, after reaching the summit of their sport? The mental edge, so critical in their pennant-winning year, proved difficult to sustain. This translated into more subtle, yet impactful, on-field struggles—perhaps a missed cut-off throw that allowed an extra base, a crucial error that extended an inning, or a consistent inability to deliver a timely hit that had characterized their 1959 heroics. The fine margins that define championships seemed to consistently elude them, turning previously comfortable victories into frustrating near-misses.

Manager Walter Alston from Darrtown, Ohio 1960 Topps card # 212 from Authiors's Dodger Museum Collection.

Guiding this challenging transition was manager Walter Alston, a man renowned for his quiet demeanor and steady hand, but his efforts were deeply supported and underpinned by the consistent and strategic leadership of Walter O'Malley, the team's President and owner. O'Malley was intimately involved in daily operations, his meticulous attention permeating every facet of the franchise. He oversaw a formidable front office that included figures like Executive VP and General Manager Emil Bavasi, a shrewd talent evaluator. Beyond player personnel, O'Malley ensured exceptional fan engagement through stable ticket prices and prompt, personalized responses to every fan inquiry, cultivating a vital sense of community. Crucially, he meticulously oversaw the business of baseball, including every detail of the continuous development of the spring training facility at Dodgertown and, most significantly, the groundbreaking construction of Dodger Stadium itself. His steady, far-sighted leadership provided an invaluable bedrock of stability and a clear vision for the future, even as the team grappled with its new reality on the field. The playing roster itself remained largely consistent, intensifying the focus on how existing stars like the fading slugger Duke Snider, the versatile Jim Gilliam, the burgeoning Maury Wills, and the powerful pitching duo of Don Drysdale and Sandy Koufax would respond to the amplified expectations, and whether they could reignite the spark of their championship season. The true battle, therefore, was often as mental as physical, a struggle to rekindle the underdog fire when the laurel wreaths of victory still seemed fresh and heavy.

The 1960 season itself proved to be the immediate and undeniable manifestation of this "hangover effect." The Dodgers finished a surprising 4th in the National League with an 82-72 record, a significant and disappointing drop from their championship form of 88-68 in 1959. Their struggles allowed other National League contenders, notably the eventual World Series champion Pittsburgh Pirates and the ascendant San Francisco Giants, to capitalize on their dip in form, intensifying the nascent rivalries of the era and signaling a shift in the league's power dynamics. While Don Drysdale commendably led the league in strikeouts with 246—a testament to his raw power and competitive fire—his 15 wins against 14 losses and a 2.84 ERA reflected the team's overall struggles, indicating a lack of consistent run support or late-game relief. Young Sandy Koufax, still inconsistent in his command but possessing an undeniable, tantalizing potential, showed increasing flashes of his future dominance with 8 wins, 13 losses, a 3.91 ERA, and a notable 197 strikeouts, truly hinting at the unparalleled greatness that lay just ahead. Like a fine wine Sandy Koufax needed to "age" or perhaps find his "sea legs" so to speak. The important thing is that experience led to success. In this case practice did make perfect. The fans were then able to see an unbelievable run of success that created the "legend of Sandy Koufax" that resounds even today.

Autographed Don Drysdale and Sandy Koufax picture from Author's Dodger Museum Collection.

On offense, Maury Wills continued his ascendance, transforming into a true leadoff threat by leading the league in stolen bases with a remarkable 50 swipes, perpetually putting pressure on opposing pitchers and catchers.

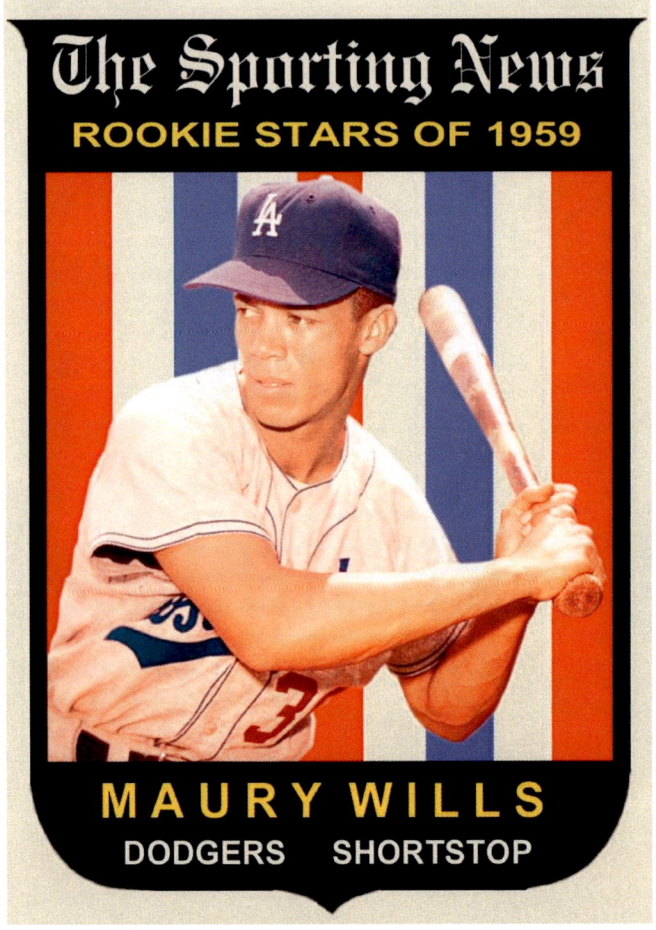

Maury Wills began his illustrious career in 1959.

Perhaps the most surprising offensive bright spot to emerge was Norm Larker, who had a stellar year at the plate, finishing second in the league in batting average with a robust .323, adding 5 home runs and 78 RBIs, becoming a consistent, reliable presence in a lineup that often struggled. However, despite these individual highlights, the overall team offensive production seemed to lack the decisive, timely punch of 1959. The Dodgers' team batting average dipped to .255 in 1960 from .268 in 1959, and their home run total dropped from 141 in 1959 to 126 in 1960, indicating a clear regression in power and situational hitting. The crisp, clutch hitting that defined their 1959 heroics seemed to elude them more often, transforming tightly contested games into frustrating losses. Even veteran slugger Duke Snider, a revered figure from the Brooklyn era, saw a noticeable decline in production, hitting 14 home runs with a .243 average, a clear step back from his peak years and a poignant symbol of the team's fading offensive might. The team's collective 3.86 ERA was only 4th best in the NL, and they scored 692 runs while allowing 671, reflecting an extremely narrow margin for error. Periods of inconsistency and faltering in crucial moments became more frequent, signaling a subtle but impactful loss of their championship edge. They might sweep a series against a contender, only to drop games to a cellar-dweller, or consistently lose one-run games that they would have won in '59, a frustrating indicator of their diminished margin for error and a symptom of their psychological burden. Yet, strikingly, as the team navigated these profound on-field challenges, Walter O'Malley's focus remained fixed on the long-term vision and modernization of the franchise.

Hartland Duke Snider Statue from Author's Dodger Museum Collection

In a testament to his visionary leadership, serious construction began on the ambitious Dodger Stadium after Labor Day. This wasn't merely a construction project; O'Malley was intricately involved in designing its revolutionary features, including the then-unheard-of concept of terraced parking lots allowing fans to park at the level of their seats, unobstructed views from all 56,000 seats by eliminating supporting pillars, and even the color-coded sections for easy navigation—all meticulously aimed at creating the ultimate, state-of-the-art fan experience. This groundbreaking philosophy would fundamentally reshape how sports stadiums were conceived and built for decades to come, moving beyond mere functional structures to become true architectural marvels designed for optimal fan comfort and engagement. Dodger Stadium, even from its inception, was conceived as an iconic symbol of modern Los Angeles, a permanent monument to the city's ascendancy.

1960 Sport Magazine All Stars, Don Drysdale and Charlie Neal from Author's Dodger Museum Collection.

This relentless commitment to a permanent, state-of-the-art home was unwavering, regardless of the immediate results on the field, and was built upon his earlier successful and often controversial land exchange where he traded the deed to the Dodgers' old home at Wrigley Field (Los Angeles) for the Chavez Ravine property, a deal that required immense political will and strategic foresight. Beyond Chavez Ravine, O'Malley actively supported the American League's expansion efforts to 10 teams in 1961, including the establishment of the Los Angeles Angels, demonstrating his commitment to the broader growth of Major League Baseball. He notably offered his congratulations to Gene Autry when Autry was approved as the Angels' owner, despite the inherent challenges of sharing the Los Angeles market territory. His international outreach was also evident, as he donated a Dodgers uniform to the Japan Baseball Hall of Fame and hosted Japanese legend Kaoru Betto at Dodgertown, signifying early efforts to globalize the game he loved. O'Malley envisioned baseball as a truly international pastime, laying diplomatic groundwork that would bear fruit in future years. While other National League teams like the eventual World Series champion Pittsburgh Pirates seized their moment, the Dodgers organization, under O'Malley's determined leadership, was concurrently laying the groundwork for a far grander future, a dynasty built on innovation and unparalleled vision.

Amidst the team's on-field recalibration, a beacon of raw power emerged, offering a tantalizing glimpse into the Dodgers' future offensive identity: Frank Howard. In his first taste of full-time big-league action, Howard, a towering figure known as "Hondo," played 117 games, tallied 448 at-bats, blasted 23 home runs, and drove in 77 RBIs while batting a respectable .268. This strong performance, showcasing prodigious power to all fields, earned him the Rookie of the Year award, a clear indication of his immense, undeniable talent. His towering physique and raw strength were a spectacle, and his prodigious home runs often traveled distances rarely seen at the time, electrifying crowds even in a year of team disappointment and inspiring a new generation of fans. Howard's individual brilliance provided a stark contrast to the collective unit's struggle with the "hangover," shining brightly amidst the team's frustrations. While O'Malley was busy building monumental infrastructure and the team wrestled with its championship aftermath, Howard represented a vibrant, powerful new force on the field, a singular bright spot in a year of relative disappointment. His electrifying debut created immense anticipation for his first full season, positioning him as a potent symbol of the team's potential rebound and future dominance, representing the future of a game that was slowly but surely embracing the power hitter, a compelling contrast to the small-ball era that had just passed and a harbinger of the offensive changes to come.

Ultimately, the 1960 season perfectly illustrates the immediate "hangover effect"—the unique challenges that invariably accompany the defense of a hard-won title. The Dodgers, though still a remarkably talented squad, found that resting on their laurels was not an option, and the intensity of being the reigning champions brought unforeseen pressures that tested their very resolve. Frank Howard's arrival was symbolic of the new blood and raw power needed to re-energize the team, immediately embodying individual excellence amidst collective struggle and pointing toward a promising future. Significantly, however, the 1960 season was also a profound testament to Walter O'Malley's extraordinary foresight. His efforts that year, from breaking ground on Dodger Stadium on September 17, 1959 and meticulously overseeing its groundbreaking design to supporting league expansion and fostering international ties, demonstrated a long-term vision that transcended immediate on-field results. These foundational efforts, alongside his earlier advocacy for professional sports administration education—which led to the Ohio University program in 1966—underscore his role as a pioneering force who built a sustainable dynasty not just on talent, but on innovative infrastructure and unparalleled business acumen. These seemingly disparate efforts—from stadium design to academic programs—were all part of a grander, integrated vision to professionalize and expand the sport, solidifying the Dodgers' position as a vanguard franchise that would set trends for decades. The lessons learned from the challenges of the 1960 season, combined with O'Malley's relentless building, would prove invaluable. The disappointment served as a powerful motivator, that would sharpen their resolve and forge the competitive edge needed for the legendary run of championships in the coming decade. As the year closed, the Dodgers entered the next chapter of their journey, with the full weight of expectation on their shoulders and a clear understanding that sustaining excellence would require relentless effort, continuous adaptation, and a visionary eye fixed firmly on the future.

1960 Dodger Yearbook celebrates Dodgers 1959 World Championship from Author's Dodger Museum Collection.

Chapter Eight

The Hangover Lingers, But the Future Beckons The 1961 Season: A Near Miss

The close of the 1960 season had left the Los Angeles Dodgers at a critical crossroads. Having plummeted to fourth place after their euphoric 1959 championship, the team, and indeed the entire city, understood that the "hangover effect" was very real. The easy confidence of reigning champions had been replaced by a sharpened focus on improvement and a quiet determination to redeem themselves. Expectations remained sky-high; fans, having tasted glory, craved more, and the players themselves felt the internal pressure to demonstrate that their 1959 triumph was the rule, not an exception. As the calendar turned to 1961, the Dodgers were not just looking to defend a title they no longer held; they were looking to reclaim their former glory and prove that 1960 was merely a stumble, not a fall. Power-hitting phenom Frank Howard, fresh off his Rookie of the Year debut that offered tantalizing glimpses of his immense potential, was poised for his first full season, a potent symbol of the raw talent ready to ignite the offense and inject new life into the lineup. He fully delivered on the promise he had shown in his late-1960 debut. In his first full season, the towering slugger played 92 games, batted a robust .296, and established himself as a premier power hitter by blasting 15 home runs and driving in 45 RBIs. Guiding this quest for redemption, Walter O'Malley, the team's visionary President and owner, continued to operate with a dual and unwavering focus: meticulously overseeing the immediate on-field product while simultaneously driving ambitious, long-term projects that would, by decade's end, solidify the Dodgers' foundational and cultural presence in Los Angeles.

The 1961 season began with a palpable sense of urgency emanating from spring training. Manager Walter Alston, a quiet but firm leader, pushed his squad, acutely aware that the National League had grown fiercely competitive, with teams like the Pittsburgh Pirates (1960 World Series champions) and the surging Cincinnati Reds now formidable contenders. The Dodgers' core remained largely intact, featuring the smooth defensive play of Maury Wills at shortstop, the consistent arm of veteran Don Drysdale, and the enigmatic talent of Sandy Koufax, who was still striving for consistency, a diamond in the rough yet to be fully polished. The bitter lessons of 1960 underscored the dire need for consistent, top-tier performance to navigate the competitive waters. O'Malley's presence remained constant and strategic, his hand evident in every facet of the organization. He continued his close oversight of the entire front office, including Executive VP and General Manager Emil Bavasi, emphasizing the meticulous business practices, proactive marketing, and dedicated fan engagement that were already hallmarks of the Dodgers. From keeping ticket prices stable to ensuring every phone call and letter from fans received a prompt response, O'Malley's attention to detail built an enduring loyalty, cementing the bond between the franchise and its rapidly growing fanbase in Southern California. This sustained, hands-on leadership provided a crucial anchor, fostering stability and a sense of shared purpose as the team navigated a demanding 154-game schedule.

Emil "Buzzie" Bavasi with Don Drysdale and Sandy Koufax

On the field, the Dodgers showed significant and undeniable improvement over their post-championship dip, transforming from a fourth-place team to a legitimate pennant contender. They finished the 1961 season in a strong second place in the National League with an 89-65 record, a marked rebound from 1960's performance, though still four games behind the surging Cincinnati Reds. The team's offense became a league leader, demonstrating renewed vitality. They scored 765 runs—the most in the NL—and launched a formidable 153 home runs. While the team batting average remained a respectable .257, the overall run production reflected a far more potent and dangerous attack than the previous year. Pitching, too, saw significant tightening, with the team ERA dropping to a much-improved 3.23. Individually, Frank Howard fully delivered on the promise he had shown in his late-1960 debut. In his first full season, the towering slugger played 92 games, batted a robust .296, and established himself as a premier power hitter by blasting 15 home runs and driving in 45 RBIs. Fans were mesmerized by the sheer force of his swings, and he became an instant favorite for his raw power, a striking contrast to the more nuanced offensive game of Wills. Meanwhile, Don Drysdale continued to be a workhorse and a reliable ace, posting a strong 13-10 record with an excellent 3.69 ERA and 182 strikeouts, consistently delivering quality starts and carrying the load for the pitching staff. Left-hander Johnny Podres notched the league's best winning percentage (.783) with an 18-5 record and a 3.74 ERA. For Podres, that was tops for games won in a season during his career. Stan Williams contributed his career high 15 wins.

1959 Morrell Meats Johnny Podres Card from Author's Dodger Museum Collection.

Stan Williams auto pix from Author's Dodger Museum Collection.

Dodger pitchers led the National League with 1,105 strikeouts. Maury Wills remained a dynamic force on the basepaths, a constant threat to opposing pitchers. He logged another impressive 35 stolen bases, though he was second in baseball to the White Sox's Luis Aparicio, his speed still set the tone for the Dodgers' aggressive style of play, often turning singles into doubles and disrupting opponent defenses. Even aging veteran slugger Duke Snider, despite a continued decline in his overall production (hitting 16 home runs with a .296 average), still contributed his veteran presence and occasional timely hit, while Jim Gilliam provided consistent versatility and solid hitting from his second base position, embodying the team's gritty resilience. Wally Moon finished the Coliseum era with a .328 batting average with 17 home runs and 88 RBI, while left-handed first baseman and outfielder Ron Fairly contributed a .322 average with 10 homers and 48 RBI.

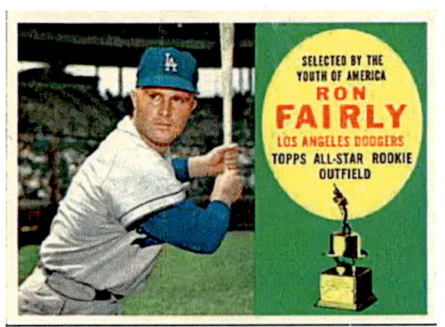

Ron Fairly Rookie Card from Author's Dodger Museum Collection.

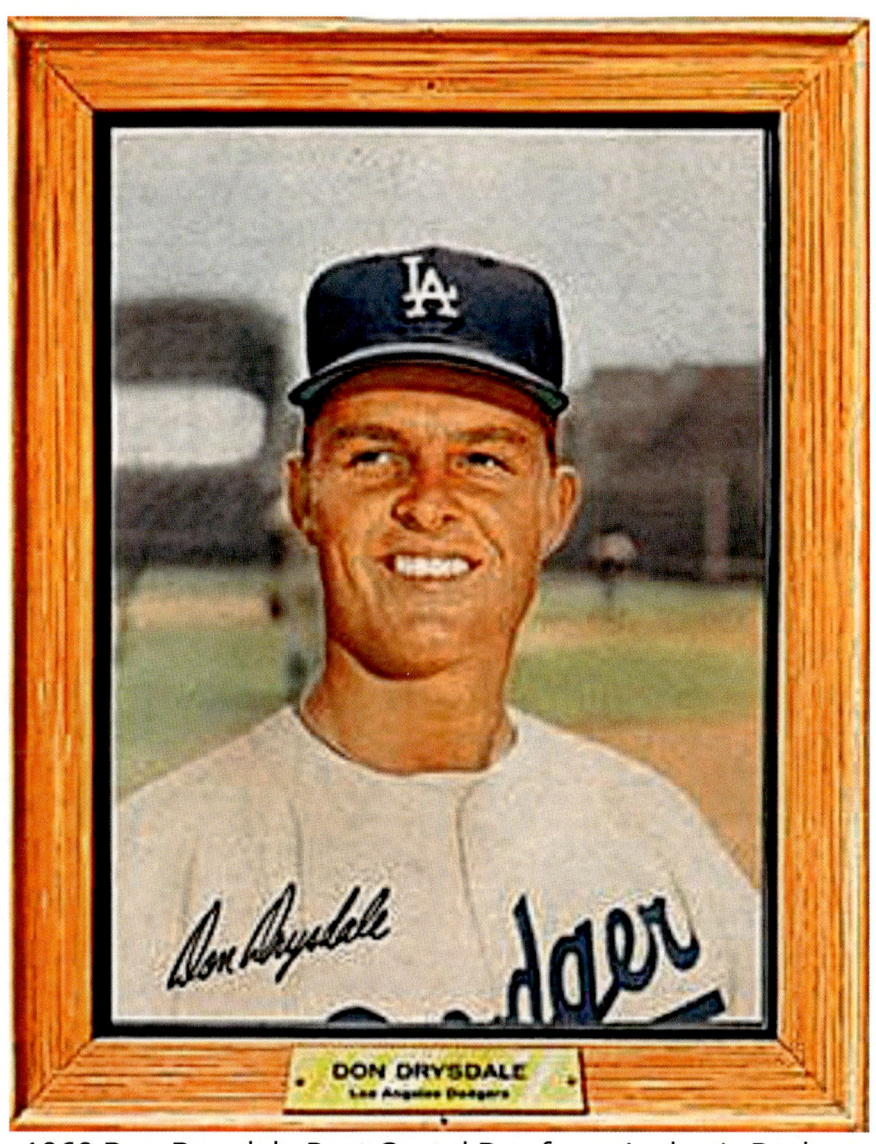

1960 Don Drysdale Post Cereal Box from Author's Dodger Museum Collection,

However, it was during the 1961 season that Sandy Koufax embarked on the most pivotal transformation of his career, a moment destined for baseball lore that would forever alter his trajectory and the Dodgers' future. Despite his undeniable talent and burgeoning strikeout numbers, Koufax had often struggled profoundly with wildness and control, a frustrating inconsistency that plagued his early years, leading to a high walk rate that often undermined his explosive pitches. His frustration reached a peak early in the 1961 spring training. Famously, during a particular exhibition game against the Minnesota Twins where Koufax walked the bases loaded, a situation that had become all too common, backup catcher Norm Sherry visited the mound. Sherry, with remarkable insight and a calm demeanor, delivered advice that would prove to be a revelation. He simply told Koufax to stop "trying to throw so hard" and instead focus on getting the ball over the plate, trusting his natural, overwhelming velocity and movement. It was a subtle tweak, a mental key rather than a mechanical overhaul, shifting Koufax's focus from overpowering hitters to simply commanding his pitches. This simple, yet profound, advice freed Koufax. While not an overnight statistical explosion, the shift in Koufax's mindset became evident as the season progressed. He began to harness his overwhelming talent with newfound control, and by the end of 1961, Koufax recorded a true breakout season, finishing with 18 wins against 13 losses, dramatically lowering his ERA to 3.52, and, remarkably, leading the entire league with an astounding 269 strikeouts. This newfound command, coupled with his already devastating fastball and curveball, signaled the true beginning of his legendary, Hall of Fame career, forever changing the landscape of National League pitching. Meanwhile, Walter O'Malley's extraordinary vision continued to materialize off the field, independent of the team's daily wins and losses. The construction of Dodger Stadium was a gargantuan task in 1961, proceeding at a relentless pace that bordered on the miraculous. The site was a hive of intense activity, with progress on his revolutionary design concepts – terraced parking lots allowing fans to drive directly to the level of their seats, unobstructed views from all 56,000 seats by eliminating supporting pillars, and even the color-coded sections for easy navigation – visibly taking shape. O'Malley famously maintained tight control over every detail, from the dimensions of the field to the concession stands, ensuring the ballpark would offer an unparalleled fan experience, a true jewel for Los Angeles. This commitment to a permanent, state-of-the-art home, a venture born from his earlier visionary land exchange of the old Wrigley Field (Los Angeles) deed for the Chavez Ravine property, was relentless. Indeed, the construction was ahead of schedule for much of 1961, a testament to his dedication and hard work.

1962 Auravision Record of Sandy Koufax from Author's Dodger Museum Collection.

The year 1961 also marked the debut of the Los Angeles Angels, who played their inaugural season. They called Wrigley Field (Los Angeles), a smaller, charming former minor league ballpark with a seating capacity of 20,457, their home for this first year, a temporary measure before they would famously become tenants at Dodger Stadium alongside the Dodgers in 1962. O'Malley, despite the new competition in the Dodgers' market, maintained a remarkably supportive stance, reflecting his belief in the overall growth of Major League Baseball in Southern California. However, a burgeoning point of contention in 1961 was O'Malley's relationship with the new American League expansion team, the Angels, owned by famed "singing cowboy" Gene Autry. While O'Malley received a substantial sum ($350,000) from Autry for territorial rights and a percentage of gate receipts as rent, there was an immediate and public disagreement over the name of the new ballpark. Gene Autry, seeking to establish the Angels' own identity, publicly announced in November 1961 that his team would refer to their new home as "Chavez Ravine" in all settings rather than "Dodger Stadium." It was an apparent attempt to differentiate his team from their landlord and stake a claim to the shared space. This set the stage for a sometimes strained relationship between the two franchises, even as O'Malley had publicly assisted Autry and welcomed him to the Los Angeles baseball scene. O'Malley once explained his position regarding the Angels' lease of Dodger Stadium in the Pasadena Star-News: "Their rent of 7 1/2 per cent of their ticket sales was 25 per cent less than the rent we paid at the Coliseum (10 per cent) before we built Dodger Stadium. When the agreement was drawn with the Angels, I wanted to be sure there was no room for criticism. A board of other major league owners was set up to review the terms. Several on this board said they would like to have such an agreement for rental in their cities when new stadiums are built...Our parking fee of $1 per car has been assailed by some critics. Also criticized was the fact that we kept the parking income from Angel games. It should be realized that this is taxed land — and that our corporation profits are also taxed. We need parking revenue to meet these obligations." Autry himself acknowledged O'Malley's assistance in bringing the expansion Angels into what would become a shared territory, telling the L.A. Herald & Express in 1961: "It was only because of his help that we were able to bring an American League team to L.A. The Angels have a tough row to hoe."

An aerial view of Holman Stadium, Dodgertown, Vero Beach, Florida, circa 1960s. Walter O'Malley created the adjacent heart-shaped lake as a valentine to his wife Kay when Holman Stadium opened in 1953.

Beyond the stadium and local territorial issues, O'Malley remained deeply involved in the overall management of the Dodgers, including the crucial spring training operations at Dodgertown in Vero Beach, Florida. Here, he addressed a lingering dispute with the City of Vero Beach over the 21-year lease of the facility, articulating the Dodgers' significant financial contributions to quell concerns. In 1961, continuing his friendship with baseball leaders in Japan, O'Malley invited the professional Tokyo Yomiuri Giants to train at Dodgertown. The Giants arrived in Vero Beach on the Dodger-owned DC-6B airplane from Los Angeles, marking the first of five team visits to Dodgertown by Yomiuri. In his first full-time job at Dodgertown, future Dodger President Peter O'Malley, Walter's son, served as liaison, making all the arrangements and schedule for the Giants from their arrival to departure. The Giants were led by Japan Baseball Hall of Fame Manager Tetsuharu Kawakami, and two of Japan's greatest Hall of Fame players – Sadaharu Oh and Shigeo Nagashima – made their first visit to Dodgertown in 1961, foreshadowing the global reach baseball would eventually achieve. On April 7, 1961, following the Giants training stay at Dodgertown, O'Malley sent a telegram with good wishes to Giants' founder and owner Matsutaro Shoriki, known as "the father of professional baseball in Japan".

Dodger minor league Manager Stan Wasiak (center) conducts infield drills with players from the Tokyo Yomiuri Giants during their 1961 spring training visit to Dodgertown, Vero Beach, Florida.

The Giants' visit was historic, as it was the first time a team from Japan at the professional level had worked out with an American major league team. O'Malley's message was prophetic as he writes, "It is my hope that your Giants and our Dodgers will both emerge victorious at the conclusion of our seasons." Yomiuri returned home and won the 1961 Japan Series, their first championship since 1955, a testament to the benefits of their groundbreaking training experience.

Peter O'Malley was named Director, Dodgertown, Vero Beach, Florida in fall, 1961 and was responsible for all business operations and Dodger spring training camps for three years (1962-1965).

It was also in 1961 that Walter's son Peter began to take on a more prominent role, being named Director of Dodgertown for the upcoming 1962 season. Peter O'Malley would later, in 1962, famously and boldly remove all segregated signs and actively encourage integration at Holman Stadium in Dodgertown, personally guiding Black fans to previously "white-only" sections, a significant step against the prevailing Jim Crow laws of the South. Dodgertown, a city within a city (Vero Beach), was Major League Baseball's first fully-integrated spring training site in the South, a profound and often overlooked aspect of the Dodgers' legacy. It is the only sports site listed on the U.S. Civil Rights Trail, whose slogan is "What happened here changed the world". These monumental behind-the-scenes efforts in 1961 were not just about building a stadium; they were about laying the concrete foundation for a modern, expansive, and globally minded baseball franchise, deeply rooted in both business acumen and progressive values.

The 1961 season, despite falling short of a pennant, was a profoundly significant year for the Los Angeles Dodgers, demonstrating a vital recovery from the previous season's "hangover." It showcased the formidable talent of Frank Howard emerging as a bona fide slugger and, most notably, bore witness to Sandy Koufax's career-altering adjustment, a revelation that foretold future greatness. This near-miss was a crucial learning experience, sharpening the team's resolve and exposing areas for further growth and refinement. Furthermore, 1961 marked the Dodgers' final season at the venerable Los Angeles Memorial Coliseum, a temporary home that had served them since their arrival in 1958, but was now giving way to their magnificent, purpose-built stadium. In the very last Dodger game at the Coliseum, on September 20, 1961, Sandy Koufax pitched all 13 innings of a thrilling 3-2 win over the Chicago Cubs, throwing an astonishing 205 pitches! The Cubs scored both their runs in the fourth inning, but Koufax struck out 15 batters, delivering a truly heroic performance that provided a fitting, if not prophetic, farewell to their temporary home. During their four seasons playing at the Coliseum, the Dodgers had no rainouts, a big factor discussed in the advantages of relocating to Los Angeles. City councilmember Roz Wyman said many times that she told O'Malley that rainouts would be a thing of the past in Los Angeles. In fact, their first Los Angeles rainout did not occur until April 21, 1967, five years into playing in Dodger Stadium. Simultaneously, Walter O'Malley's unwavering commitment to building that state-of-the-art facility and expanding baseball's reach solidified the organizational pillars necessary for sustained success. The combined efforts on and off the field during 1961 positioned the Dodgers on the precipice of an era that would redefine baseball championships for years to come, with their permanent, spectacular home on the horizon. Ultimately, 1961 for Walter O'Malley was a year dominated by the visionary pursuit of his dream stadium, tempered by the persistent reverberations of past controversies, the complex realities of operating a major league baseball team in a still-segregated nation, and the budding territorial squabbles with a new cross-town rival intent on forging its own identity.

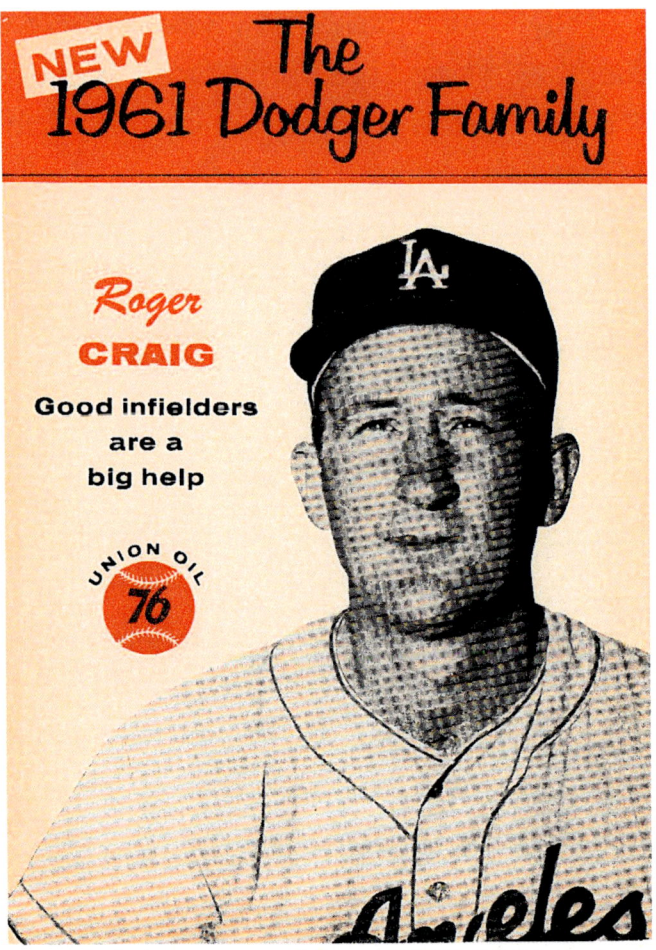

At each homestand from 1960-1961 these booklets were given away, a total of 50 different. All 50 are in Author's Dodger Museum Collection,

These 2 1/2-inch pins were sold at the Coliseum in 1960 and 1961 from Author's Dodger Museum Collection.

Photo Gallery

This original Dodger Stadium model was created by Warner Bros. Studio using design plans and colors as a gift for Walter O'Malley from Hollywood producer-director Mervyn LeRoy and was used as a conference table in O'Malley's office. The model was on public display in 1960-61, including exhibits at home shows, Bank of America in downtown Los Angeles and in Riverside, the Los Angeles County Fair in Pomona, and lobby of the Los Angeles Mirror newspaper.

(Back) Walter O'Malley sits in his Coliseum box for a 1961 game with producer-director Mervyn LeRoy, Jimmy and Gloria Stewart. Actor Stewart's career spanned some 80 films and numerous industry awards as well as the Presidential Medal of Freedom. LeRoy is best known for producing the 1939 film The Wizard of Oz.

ALLEN SCHERY

January 28, 1962, Walter O'Malley was honored by the Beverly Hills B'nai B'rith, a Jewish fraternal and charitable organization, as its "1961 Man of the Year". (L-R): Seated – Walter Alston and Los Angeles business leader Chad McClellan. Standing – Sandy Koufax, Don Drysdale, Walter O'Malley and Leo Durocher. At the gala dinner headed by producer-director Mervyn LeRoy, honorary coaches were Milton Berle, Nat King Cole, Tony Curtis, Gene Autry, Kirk Douglas, Dean Martin, Rosalind Russell, Dinah Shore, Edward G. Robinson, Jimmy Stewart, Casey Stengel, Jack L. Warner, Leo Durocher,

George Burns, Joe E. Brown, Jack Benny plus Danny Kaye and entertainment co-chair Sammy Cahn.

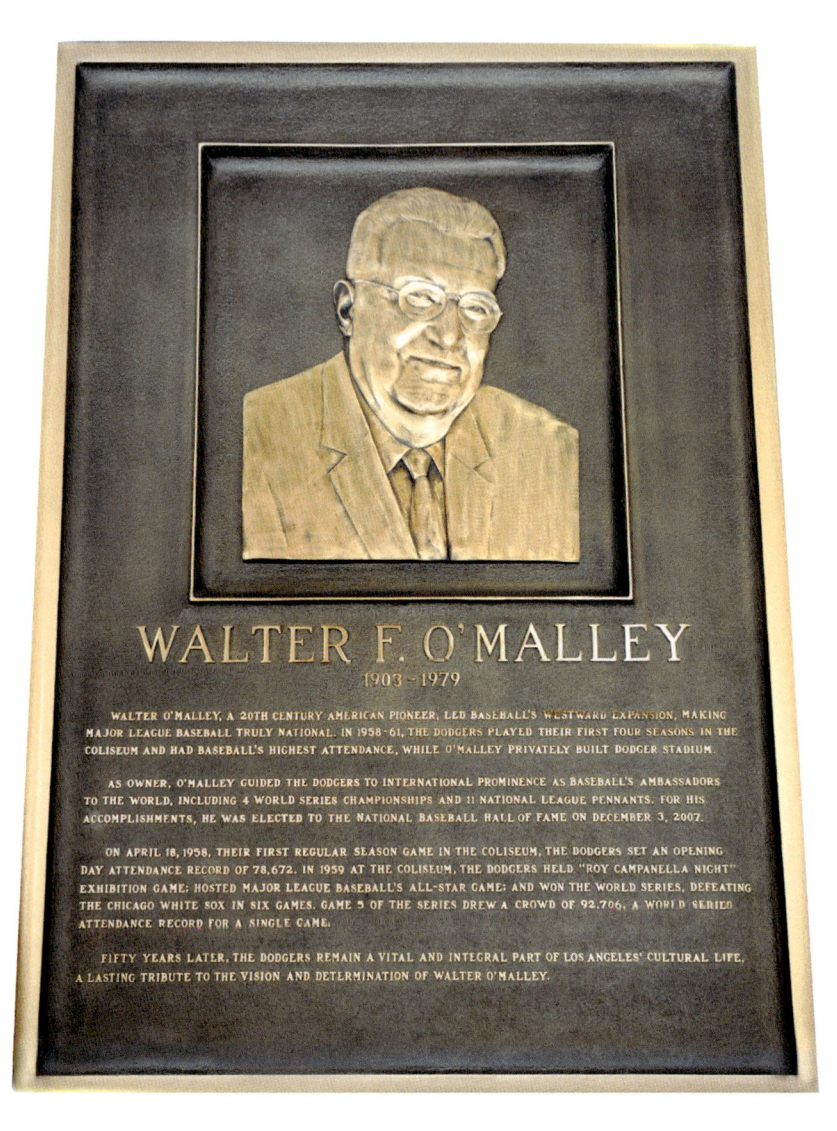

Plaque erected at Coliseum to commemorate Walter O'Malley.

Chapter Nine

The Challenges of Building Dodger Stadium

For Walter O'Malley, pursuing a permanent home for the Los Angeles Dodgers was as monumental a task as assembling a championship team. While the Dodgers temporarily played at the expansive Los Angeles Memorial Coliseum from 1958 to 1961, O'Malley knew a long-term, custom-built baseball facility was vital for the franchise's future in Southern California. His vision was not just for a ballpark but a meticulously planned sports complex that would redefine the fan experience. On November 21, 1956, findings of a joint study by the L.A. Department of Recreation and Parks and the City Planning Department about possible sites and the most suitable location for a Major League Baseball Park in Los Angeles were released. L.A. City Council requested a joint study in July 1956. In the findings of the study, it states, "Consideration was given to the possibility of other suitable sites, however none was found within the city with qualifications meriting serious consideration." As to the Chavez Ravine site, the study noted, "The rugged topography of this area does not appear to be desirable for the proposed use. Although it is possible to design a major league baseball park with essential large flat surfaces, and necessary parking areas, such facilities would involve extensive earthwork and retaining walls. Most of the property considered for this use is owned by the City of Los Angeles and is vacant. Abutting land is in private ownership and, except for a few small residences, is vacant." O'Malley's efforts would lead him to the City of Los Angeles's involvement with Chavez Ravine and its deeply intertwined themes of civic progress, political maneuvering, community displacement, and deeply held promises beginning in 1949, long before any Dodger relocation queries.

The Federal Housing Act of 1949 created funding for public housing projects in cities. On August 8, 1949, the Los Angeles City Council unanimously agreed with the federally sponsored City Housing Authority to construct 10,000 units. In 1950, the Housing Authority of the City of Los Angeles, a federal agency of the U.S. government, authorized a housing project for Chavez Ravine. Residents were notified that their properties would be appraised, and they would receive compensation, with priority rights to the new "Elysian Park Heights" units. By 1952, 99.9% of the residents accepted and relocated. This was long before a Dodger move was even imagined. Those who refused remained on their property illegally and did not pay property taxes. Chavez Ravine was then one of 11 L.A. housing projects.

HOUSING AUTHORITY OF THE CITY OF LOS ANGELES

July 24, 1950

To The Families of The Palo Verde and Chavez Ravine Areas:

This letter is to inform you that a public housing development will be built on this location for families of low income. The attached map shows the property that is going to be used. The house you are living in is included.

Within a short time surveyors will be working in your neighborhood. Later you will be visited by representatives of the Housing Authority, who will ask you to allow them to inspect your house in order to estimate its value. Title investigators will also visit you. You should be sure that any person who comes to your house has proper identification.

It will be several months at least before your property is purchased. After the property is bought, the Housing Authority will give you all possible assistance in finding another home. If you are eligible for public housing, you will have top priority to move into any of our public housing developments. Later you will have the first chance to move back into the new Elysian Park Heights development.

Three offices are being opened in this area to give you information and answers to your questions. They are located as follows:

Santo Nino Parochial Hall at 1034 Effie St., (rear of Church)
San Conrado Mission at 1809 Bouett, (near Amador St.)
Tony Visco's old grocery store at 1035 Lilac Terrace

You are welcome to come in at any time. We will be open day and night this week, July 24 through July 28, and during the day Saturday, July 29. Next week we will be open during the day and in the evenings by appointment. Telephone ANgelus 2-1963 for any information.

We want to assure you that it is our intention to help you and work with you in every way possible.

Yours very truly,

Sidney Green
Management Supervisor

The saga of Chavez Ravine long predated the Dodgers' arrival in Los Angeles. Before the 1950s, Chavez Ravine was home to three distinct, self-sufficient, and predominantly Mexican-American communities – La Loma, Palo Verde, and Bishop. These were neighborhoods characterized by families, small homes, churches, and schools, creating a vibrant cultural enclave in the hills north of downtown Los Angeles. Despite their proximity to a burgeoning metropolis, these communities maintained an almost rural feel, a quiet corner where some families had established a unique way of life. In July 1950, under the banner of urban renewal and a federal program to address the post-war housing crisis, the City of Los Angeles embarked on the Elysian Park Heights public housing project. The city initiated eminent domain proceedings to acquire the privately owned land in Chavez Ravine for this planned development. Residents were given notices to vacate, and all but a few, trusting the city's promise of new, affordable housing, sold their properties and relocated. Three government appraisers appraised each property, with the highest valuation assigned after court review. The homes were then demolished, leaving large swaths of the ravine cleared.

However, political winds soon shifted. In 1953, amidst the intense Joseph McCarthy era, a growing anti-communist sentiment often conflated public housing projects with "socialism." A new city administration, led by Mayor Norris Poulson, came into power. Poulson, who ran against public housing in 1953, was elected as the new L.A. mayor. The Elysian Park Heights project, along with vast amounts of land already acquired and cleared, effectively stalled. Vacant, denuded hillsides largely replaced the previously vibrant communities.

At that time, Dodger owner Walter O'Malley's sole focus was on finding a solution to replacing aging Ebbets Field and its limited parking, with a privately built and financed stadium in Brooklyn. During his unprecedented 10-year effort, O'Malley wanted to build and privately finance baseball's first dome stadium at his preferred location at the intersection of Atlantic and Flatbush Avenues in Brooklyn, today the site of Barclays Center. It was only after all of O'Malley's options were exhausted in New York that he considered Los Angeles in earnest in 1957. When O'Malley visited L.A. in May 1957 and flew in a two-seat Sheriff's helicopter over Chavez Ravine seeing the land from above for the first time, he had no idea that there were a few squatters still on the land. L.A. officials recognized the opportunity to obtain big league ball.

For seven years, the land sat empty and neglected, a desolate monument to failed urban planning. Mayor Poulson negotiated with the U.S. government to repurchase the land for $1,279,000, an amount below what the government spent initially but with a "public purpose" clause. This repurchase meant the land was no longer federally designated for public housing. The City of Los Angeles then owned the land in Chavez Ravine. For years, Poulson and the City Council struggled with how to use the largely barren and hilly area. Several ideas were floated, including a zoo, cemetery, artificial lake, state college, expansion of the Police Academy, golf courses, and a city park. If any of the above were to be developed, funds would have to be allocated by a vote of the City Council, and, at the time, there was nothing in the budget for any of these projects.

In this complex and politically charged landscape, Walter O'Malley, searching desperately for a permanent home for his Dodgers, entered the picture in 1957. Chavez Ravine emerged as the most viable option. The city, saddled with a large, publicly owned, and now largely vacant tract of land designated for public use but unable to proceed with its original plan, saw an opportunity to permanently bring Major League Baseball, a powerful symbol of a burgeoning modern city, to Los Angeles. In September 1957, a land exchange agreement, negotiated by Chad McClellan on behalf of the City and County of Los Angeles and O'Malley, was reached. (McClellan, a highly respected Los Angeles business leader, served as the Under Secretary of Commerce for International Affairs for the Eisenhower Administration). O'Malley would surrender the Dodgers' private ownership of the historically significant Wrigley Field in Los Angeles (appraised in 1957 at $2.25 million) to the city. In return, the city would grant the Dodgers 300 acres of the Chavez Ravine land. The agreement stipulated that O'Malley would privately finance and build and maintain the 50,000-seat stadium. He committed to constructing and donating additional recreational facilities (playgrounds, baseball fields) for public use on the remaining city land at an initial $500,000 and $60,000 annual payments for 20 years. In addition, it put the land back on the tax rolls with an initial $345,000 in property taxes that O'Malley had to pay.

The proposed deal immediately ignited a fierce public and political debate. Opponents, ranging from civic groups to labor unions and residents' advocates, characterized the city as using public land for private enterprise. They argued it was the city's eminent domain abuse, betraying the original intent for public housing. Proponents, including the city administration and business leaders, countered that the deal would bring immense public and economic benefits (including property taxes, jobs, and income to area businesses), put a major league team permanently in Los Angeles, and transform a "blighted" and underutilized area into a productive civic asset, all without direct taxpayer funding for the stadium itself. Every aspect of the city's agreement with the Dodgers was approved by the City Council, Los Angeles voters, and the courts (including the California Supreme Court).

The fate of the Dodgers' move, and the stadium deal ultimately came down to a city-wide referendum (Proposition B) held on June 3, 1958. It was a hard-fought campaign, often described as a "battle for the soul of Los Angeles." The city was cleaved, with passionate arguments on radio, in newspapers, and door-to-door. It was not merely about baseball but a referendum on the city's future, the role of private enterprise versus public good, and the ethics of eminent domain. The "Save Our Dodgers" campaign highlighted the pride and economic benefits of major league baseball. In contrast, the "No Dodger Stadium" campaign, spearheaded by Pacific Coast League San Diego Padres owners, including J.A. Smith, emphasized concerns about public land, broken promises, and the implications for residents. Padres' President James F. Mulvaney and Ralph Kiner, Padres' General Manager, wrote in a November 5, 1957, joint letter to O'Malley, "As we have previously told you, we have everything to lose and nothing to gain if the referendum is successful and, therefore, definitely have no interest, whatsoever, in its success." Jerald Podair explains in his book City of Dreams: "Much of the committee's financial backing came from the Smith brothers, J.A. and C. Arnholt, of San Diego, where the latter owned the local Pacific Coast League baseball team. The team's fortunes would certainly suffer from the presence of the Dodgers in nearby Los Angeles. The Smiths' obvious economic interest in defeating the Dodger contract made it imperative that their support for the Citizens Committee be obscured. The brothers were hardly representative of the people for which the committee claimed to speak."

From Southern California Quarterly, fall 1980, "Los Angeles and the Dodger War, 1957-1962" by Cary S. Henderson, "Since building a municipal baseball stadium was politically impossible, Los Angeles could offer only land and $2,000,000 for access roads. It must also be noted that the land in Chavez Ravine had never been considered valuable until O'Malley was attracted to it as a stadium site. The rough terrain seemed unattractive to everyone else who looked at it. Walt Disney, for example, refused to consider it as a site for his projected Disneyland. In a sense, then, it was O'Malley and the use he planned for the land that made the property valuable, whatever its potential could have been for others...The 'public purpose' served by municipal ballparks is to generate money through rents, concessions, and parking charges. The Dodgers have compensated by their annual local taxes."

Despite intense opposition and 677,581 votes cast, the referendum passed by a narrow margin of 25,785 votes, granting legal approval for the land exchange. L.A.'s 9th District, which covered the Chavez Ravine area, Boyle Heights, Bunker Hill, Civic Center, Chinatown, Little Tokyo, and the Central Avenue corridor and was represented by City Councilmember Ed Roybal, had one of the largest margins of approval for the Proposition B referendum. This democratic mandate, though slim, was crucial for O'Malley, providing a foundation for the project to move forward. Ergo, by law, it was now the people's mandate.

However, the legal and human challenges were far from over. A tiny number of families had never left Chavez Ravine, holding onto the original promise of public housing or simply refusing to abandon their properties despite authorities sending repeated eviction notices that they ignored. One resident Ruth Rayford, a trained actress who studied at the Perry School of Dramatic Arts in St. Louis, had been instructed to look upset by the eviction. "The television man told us to look fierce, and I thought it would be fun, so I raised my cane and did the best I could. We knew the time would come when we would have to move, so we didn't mind too much. We should have done it sooner, and then we would have been settled by now," she told the Los Angeles Examiner on May 15, 1959. This once again proves William Randolph Hearst's time worn phrase that the press needs to comfort the afflicted and afflict the comfortable. Real stories get swallowed using these false premises but sell papers. These were the last 12 "holdouts" (as 99.9 percent of the other residents had long left the area), and their plight became the emotional epicenter of the controversy. By 1959, when construction of Dodger Stadium was to start, the city, which had every opportunity in intervening years to clear the land and present it whole to the Dodgers, had to evict these remaining residents, who had ignored repeated eviction notices. The city of Los Angeles was scrambling at the last minute to clear the final "holdouts", a job that should have been achieved years before, no matter what purpose the land was to be used. The Dodgers were NOT complicit with the city of Los Angeles in the removal. That was solely the city's responsibility and up to that point it had failed. Their fierce attachment to their homes, a profound sense of injustice, and broken trust in the city fueled their unwavering resistance. They felt betrayed by a system that had initially forced them to sell for one public purpose only to see the land repurposed for another though all was done in a very public forum and with necessary City Council votes despite the referendum's outcome and subsequent court orders, these families resisted eviction, leading to highly publicized confrontations. In his May 6, 1959, letter to "The Mailbag" of the Los Angeles Mirror News, "holdout" resident Manuel Arechiga wrote, "I haven't anything against the Dodgers but if they want my land let them pay a reasonable price for it, not take it away. I am 72 and cannot buy a house for the price they offer me and stay out of debt. I have two houses and three lots, and they offer me $10,050." Seven years prior, after reviewing three independent appraisals and picking the highest amount for the land, the Superior Court then put that amount in escrow for the family. That amount was determined during the city's 1950 public housing project (which failed in 1953) and had nothing to do with the Dodgers. From historian and author Nathan Marsak who has written extensively on the topic: "The Dodger corporation was in no way involved in removing people who had lost their homes years before (yes, that includes the Arechigas). We are told we must 'hold the Dodgers accountable for their part in destroying Palo Verde, La Loma and Bishop!' But no...we don't. Because Dodger Corp. were not 'complicit' with the city in destroying one single house. If they were, then, when and how? Exactly: didn't happen." Unfortunately, in the human experience people seem to gravitate towards conspiracy theories despite the lack of evidence. These events graphically prove that assertion. Add to that the "Hearst" necessity to sell papers and we have a toxic mix of gobbledy gook.

The most poignant images of this resistance occurred on May 8th, 1959, when Los Angeles County Sheriff's deputies arrived to enforce court-ordered repeated eviction notifications. While the number of resisting families was miniscule relative to the 300-acre site (most of which was already cleared and vacant), their forced removal etched a permanent mark on the city's memory and became a cautionary tale about urban development. The fact that this was a Hearst technique used to sell newspapers was lost on the public. On May 11, 1959, the "holdout" Arechiga family appeared before the Los Angeles City Council and was granted a public hearing. They made it sound as if they were destitute and had no place to live but were of no mind to accept charity. However, arrangements were made for them to live in public housing quarters at no expense to them, but they again refused to leave Chavez Ravine and continued living in tents. From Forever Blue, by Michael D'Antonio, "Led by sixty-seven-year-old Manuel Arechiga, the evicted residents refused to leave. Instead, they pitched tents and announced they would stay the night. Supporters arrived and by evening forty people gathered around campfires. Their city councilman, Edward Roybal, visited to offer his outrage over an act he deemed 'very cruel,' and Mr. Arechiga complained that he had been offered $10,500 for a house worth $17,000." Two days later on May 13, 1959, newspaper reports revealed that the Arechiga family owned 11 other homes at a value of more than $75,000, including "an unoccupied house located not far from their illegally established camp site in Chavez Ravine..." The next day's Los Angeles Times' headline stated, "11 L.A. Homes Owned by Chavez Evictees". On May 15, 1959, from the Los Angeles Examiner editorial and Mayor Norris Poulson's comments about the Arechiga family, "It is perfectly plain now," he said, "that the family needs no sympathy. It is a victim of its own eagerness to extract from the taxpayers more than it was granted by valid court decisions." The editorial states, "His comments on the shocking disclosures that the family owns some 11 other homes valued at more than $75,000 burned away much of the oratorical underbrush that has sprung up around this incident. Those leading the fight in the (City) Council to defy the legal eviction order are the very ones who, with respect to the Dodger agreement, set themselves above a majority of the Council, a vote of the electorate, the State Legislature, the Governor and two unanimous rulings by the State Supreme Court." Immediately, sympathy waned when the truth was revealed. Five years later on May 12, 1962, the Arechiga family still had not collected a check in excess of $10,000 from the City Housing Authority, according to Director Howard Holtzendorff. "The money has been on deposit for her (Abrana Arechiga) since 1953," he said in an article in the Los Angeles Times. The circumstances of these evictions were widely reported, with O'Malley's camp emphasizing the legal framework under which they occurred and the long-term benefits the stadium brought to the city.

  Despite the persistent protests and legal challenges, the construction of Dodger Stadium officially began with a groundbreaking ceremony on September 17, 1959. O'Malley's vision for a privately financed, state-of-the-art facility was unwavering. His detailed involvement in the stadium's design, from the unique terraced parking lots allowing fans to walk directly to their seating level to the elimination of support pillars for unobstructed views from all 56,000 seats and even the selection of the distinctive pastel seating colors for aesthetic appeal and easy navigation, reflected his commitment to an unparalleled fan experience. He selected the "world's largest scoreboards"; wide seats, the most modern lighting for night games, and there were more restrooms (48) than any other stadium, equally split for women and men. O'Malley even included dugout box seats right behind home plate, an idea that spawned from Korakuen Stadium in Tokyo during the Dodgers 1956 Goodwill Tour to Japan. The immense engineering challenge of transforming the steep, uneven terrain of Chavez Ravine into a multi-tiered stadium with precise sightlines was a monumental undertaking. Millions of cubic yards of earth were moved, and innovative techniques were employed to terrace the hillsides, creating a multi-tiered structure that seemed to grow organically from the landscape. The innovative engineering and design solutions employed during its construction were widely lauded.

Dodger Stadium was to be family-friendly, spotlessly clean and a safe environment for all. However, the path to completion was fraught with significant delays and Herculean engineering challenges. Although O'Malley had initially hoped for a 1961 opening, protracted legal battles immediately entangled the path forward. Following the narrow passage of the 1958 referendum, opponents swiftly filed lawsuits, (Kirschbaum vs. City of Los Angeles and Ruben v. City of Los Angeles), challenging the legality of the land exchange. This legal challenge immediately triggered a preliminary injunction, effectively freezing the transfer of land and preventing any physical construction. The parallel cases were consolidated and ascended through the courts, culminating in a critical California State Supreme Court ruling. It was not until January 13, 1959, that the Supreme Court unanimously upheld the contract's validity, finally clearing the primary legal hurdle. The U.S. Supreme Court denied certiorari and dismissed the case trying to block the previously approved city contract with the Dodgers on October 19, 1959. All lawsuits ended and the Dodgers took control of the land. This lengthy process, including the subsequent weeks required for the final contract to be signed in June 1959, significantly pushed back the start of physical construction from O'Malley's initial timetable. Once work finally commenced on the rugged, hilly terrain of Chavez Ravine, the scale of the undertaking was immense. Over eight million cubic yards of earth had to be moved to create the stadium bowl and its vast parking lots, which involved relocating mountains. Specialized equipment was often required, including a custom-built, 120-foot crane capable of precisely placing 40-ton precast concrete units, of which over 21,000 were used to form the stadium's framework. The challenging terrain, inclement weather, weighty rains, and associated landslides in early 1962 as the opening date loomed further complicated the already tight 19-month construction timeline. The relentless downpours led to a $500,000 cost overage, a sum that included extraordinary measures such as famously bringing a jet engine drying machine onto the field to dry the turf for sodding. Despite these formidable obstacles and a frenetic, round-the-clock push that saw O'Malley personally driving the effort and sending urgent telegrams days before opening, his resolute determination ensured the stadium would open on its revised target date.

Walter O'Malley at construction site of Dodger Stadium.

During Dodger Stadium construction, concrete pieces in varying sizes were cast on the property and a special $150,000 one-time use crane was assembled at the stadium site to move the pieces precisely into place.

ALLEN SCHERY

From the air one can easily see where eventual seating will be as it is being carved into the ravine.

The story of Chavez Ravine and Dodger Stadium is a complex tapestry woven with threads of visionary leadership, civic ambition and legal battles. Walter O'Malley believed sincerely that he was building a privately financed jewel for Los Angeles, a commitment validated by a public vote and a deal that included public recreational facilities. His perspective emphasized that the land was largely vacant and acquired by the city through eminent domain for a failed public project years before the Dodgers' involvement. For some of the displaced residents of the that failed public housing project, however, it was a profound loss of home, community, and trust, a painful episode of what they perceived as broken promises by the City of Los Angeles. Nevertheless, from the dust of controversy and the dedication of countless workers,

Dodger Stadium rose, a gleaming monument that would open its gates in 1962, becoming a beloved landmark and a symbol of Los Angeles's arrival as a major league city, forever standing as a testament to both the power of vision and the enduring weight of history.

From author Neil J. Sullivan's, The Dodgers Move West: "The interpretation which argues that Walter O'Malley orchestrated events in Los Angeles by manipulating the officials of that city ignores the highly pertinent histories both of baseball and the public housing controversy in Southern California. The overemphasis on O'Malley's role misses the vital contribution of major political actors in Los Angeles to the transfer of the Dodgers. The city council vote on October 7, 1957, culminated a concerted effort by city leaders to overcome formidable opposition to the final contract. Poulson, Wyman, McClellan, and others faced legal, political, and economic constraints similar or identical to those confronting New York officials. In Los Angeles those obstacles were overcome not because they were less imposing, nor even because the city's officials were uniquely skilled; rather, Poulson and the other advocates were committed to attracting the Dodgers, while their counterparts in New York were indifferent or hostile to the measures necessary for keeping the team. When New York realized that the threat from Los Angeles was real, officials renewed efforts to keep the Dodgers in Brooklyn, or at least in a nearby community. Until those efforts were fully spent, Los Angeles could not be sure that the arduously constructed proposal for Walter O'Malley would finally succeed."

This struggle for a new home in Los Angeles was, in many ways, a striking echo of the political problems Walter O'Malley had faced in Brooklyn, which ultimately precipitated the Dodgers' move west. In New York, O'Malley's persistent efforts to replace the aging Ebbets Field with a modern, privately financed stadium had repeatedly been stymied by the influential political figure Robert Moses. O'Malley proposed a new domed stadium in downtown Brooklyn, seeking a similar land acquisition arrangement from the city to clear existing commercial and residential areas. However, Moses, with his grand vision for public works and an insistence on public ownership of sports venues, refused to grant O'Malley the land or the cooperation he deemed necessary, often prioritizing public projects over private enterprise. This deadlock in Brooklyn, fueled by conflicting visions for urban development and O'Malley's steadfast desire to privately finance, build, and maintain a new stadium for the Dodgers, eventually led him to seek a new location. He had no desire for a publicly owned stadium.

Thus, the controversies in Chavez Ravine, though unique in their specific context of pre-existing eminent domain and a public referendum, mirrored the fundamental challenges O'Malley faced: Robert Moses blocking his privately funded stadium ambitions, leading to bitter public and political disputes over land acquisition and urban planning. Such political friction, driven by competing interests, differing visions for urban space, and the inherent complexities of involving public land and private enterprise, is an almost inescapable component of large-scale civic projects, often a testament to the very nature of human governance and diverse community needs. The successful construction of Dodger Stadium in Los Angeles represented a hard-won victory in a long-standing battle that had previously ended in his Brooklyn defeat and the team's historic relocation.

CHAVEZ RAVINE/DODGER STADIUM TIMELINE:

1949 – the Federal Housing Act was created to provide funding to cities for public housing projects.

1950 – L.A. Housing Authority authorizes a housing project in Chavez Ravine.

1950 – Residents are notified that their dwellings would be appraised and receive compensation with priority rights to the new "Elysian Park Heights" units.

1952 – 99% of the residents accepted and relocated and those who refused remained on their properties.

1953 – for political reasons the housing project failed, and the few remaining residents refused to leave.

1953-1959 – the land lay dormant for seven years.

1957 – the city of L.A. introduced Chavez Ravine to the Dodgers.

1959 – after repeatedly being told to vacate, the last handful had to leave to clear the land for construction of Dodger Stadium.

1962 – Dodger Stadium opens April 10.

Chapter Ten
The Pioneers of the New Frontier

1958 Arrivals

The very first year in Los Angeles saw the arrival of a few fresh faces, eager to make their mark on a team still finding its footing. These players, while young, immediately hinted at the future direction of the franchise.

Frank Howard (Born 1936, Debuted 1958): The Behemoth with a Bat.

"Hondo," as he was affectionately known, was an imposing figure even as a young man. At 6'7" and over 250 pounds, he was a towering presence at the plate, and his prodigious power was undeniable. Debuting in 1958 at just 21 years old, Howard offered a tantalizing glimpse of the future. While his early years were marked by flashes of brilliance interspersed with struggles to find consistent contact and a noticeable strikeout rate, his monstrous home runs quickly made him a fan favorite in the spacious confines of the Los Angeles

Memorial Coliseum – a ballpark notorious for its short left field that sometimes made his towering blasts seem commonplace. In his 1960 rookie season, Howard blasted 23 home runs, finished a close second in the National League Rookie of the Year voting, and posted an impressive .818 OPS. His raw power would be a staple of the Dodgers' offense for years to come, signaling a definitive shift towards a more power-oriented lineup. Howard would go on to hit 176 home runs in eight seasons with the Dodgers.

Ron Fairly (Born 1938, Debuted 1958): The Versatile Rookie.

Fairly, a versatile infielder and outfielder, also arrived in 1958 at the age of 20. His ability to play multiple positions made him an invaluable asset for manager Walter Alston. Over his 12 seasons with the Dodgers, Fairly played first base (486 games), right field (470 games), and left field (226 games), showcasing his defensive flexibility and reliable glovework. While not a power hitter like Howard, Fairly possessed a keen batting eye and the ability to hit for average. In 1959, he appeared in 118 games and hitting 4 home runs with 23 RBIs. His consistent presence in the lineup provided stability and his defensive flexibility allowed Alston to experiment with various configurations. Fairly's quiet professionalism and steady play made him a dependable contributor in the Dodgers' new home.

The Influx of Talent: 1959-1960.

The years immediately following the initial move saw an even greater influx of young talent, many of whom would become absolute cornerstones of the Dodgers' success, profoundly shaping the team's identity for the next decade.

Tommy Davis (Born 1939, Debuted 1959): The Hitting Machine.

When Brooklyn native Tommy Davis debuted in 1959 at just 20 years old, it was clear the Dodgers had something special. Davis possessed an incredibly smooth swing and an uncanny ability to spray line drives to all fields. His arrival immediately boosted the Dodgers' offense, providing consistent hitting from the outfield. By 1962, he had fully arrived, leading the National League in batting average with an astounding .346, collecting 230 hits (a franchise record that still stands) and driving in 153 runs (another franchise record that still stands). He followed that up with another batting title in 1963, hitting .326. Davis's consistent contact and prodigious ability to drive in runs quickly made him one of the most feared hitters in the league, a crucial component of the Dodgers' offensive strategy. Over his eight seasons with the Dodgers, he maintained a remarkable .304 batting average.

Willie Davis (Born 1940, Debuted 1960): The Speed Demon.

Willie Davis, another outfielder, arrived in 1960 at the age of 20, bringing an electrifying element to the Dodgers' game: blazing speed. His ability to cover vast amounts of ground in the outfield with effortless grace and his prowess on the basepaths instantly transformed the Dodgers' defensive and offensive capabilities. In his 4 seasons with the Dodgers, Willie Davis stole 335 bases, becoming the franchise's all-time leader in that category. He also set a club record with 1952 games played. While his bat was still developing in these early years, and he occasionally made gaffes on the basepaths typical of young speedsters, his elite speed alone created problems for opposing teams, and his defense was Gold Glove caliber. Willie Davis was a crucial component of the "speed and defense" philosophy that would become a hallmark of the Dodgers in the 1960s, contributing significantly to their 1963 and 1965 World Series championships.

Phil Ortega (Born 1939, Debuted 1960): A Young Arm for the Rotation.

As the Dodgers looked to solidify their pitching staff, Phil Ortega, a right-handed pitcher, made his debut in 1960 at 20 years old. While not yet a frontline starter, Ortega offered a promising arm and depth to a pitching staff that was already home to burgeoning aces like Sandy Koufax and Don Drysdale. Phil Ortega in 1962 appeared in 24 games, starting 3 with a 0-2 record with a 6.88 ERA. Ortega was 7-13 in 5 seasons with the Dodgers,

Walter O'Malley surveys the Coliseum.

Various Era Rookie Cards from Author's Dodger Museum Collection.

The Pivotal Role of the Ballparks: Shaping Team Identity.

The transition from Brooklyn to Los Angeles presented a unique challenge and opportunity for the Dodgers, largely dictated by their initial and permanent homes.

The Los Angeles Memorial Coliseum (1958-1961) was a truly unorthodox baseball venue. Its short left field (approximately 250 feet with a towering 42-foot screen) made it a hitter's paradise for right-handed sluggers, favoring players like Frank Howard who could reach its inviting dimensions. Games played there were often high-scoring and peculiar, forcing the team to adapt to its quirks. However, this temporary solution was quickly overshadowed by the majesty of their new permanent home.

The opening of Dodger Stadium in 1962 was a game-changer. With its symmetrical, spacious outfield and generous dimensions, it was designed as a pitcher's park, perfectly complementing the Dodgers' emerging strengths. This new environment fundamentally suited the "speed and defense" philosophy being forged by players like Willie Davis, allowing them to excel defensively and stretch singles into doubles. Critically, it also became the ideal stage for their budding aces, Sandy Koufax and Don Drysdale, to truly dominate, solidifying the team's identity as one built on pitching, defense, and opportunistic hitting.

The Final Wave Before the Peak: 1962-1963 Arrivals.

The year 1962, which culminated in a thrilling pennant race and a World Series victory, saw the arrival of a few more key young players. The 1963 World Series championship season continued this trend, showcasing the ongoing commitment to youth development.

Joe Moeller (Born 1943, Debuted 1962): The Teenage Pitcher.

Remarkably, Joe Moeller made his debut in 1962 at just 19 years old, making him one of the youngest players in the league. As a right-handed pitcher, he provided additional depth and a glimpse into the future of the Dodgers' rotation. In his debut season, he pitched 24 innings across 6 games (4 starts), earning a 1-2 record. While his contributions in 1962 were limited, his presence signaled the Dodgers' continued commitment to developing homegrown pitching talent. Moeller would go on to pitch in 174 games for the Dodgers over seven seasons, including a career-high 29 starts in 1966.

Ken McMullen (Born 1942, Debuted 1962): The Infield Prospect.

An infielder, Ken McMullen also debuted in 1962 at the age of 20. He offered defensive versatility in the infield, a valuable asset for a team that prioritized strong defense. Ken McMullen played in just six games in 1962. He played six seasons for the Dodgers over two different stints and appeared in 234 games.

Pete Richert (Born 1939, Debuted 1962): A Timely Addition to the Bullpen.

Pete Richert, a left-handed pitcher, debuted in 1962 at 22 years old. While slightly older than some of his youthful counterparts, Pete Richert played in 19 games in 1962 and was 5-4 with a 3.87 ERA. His left-handed arm provided a crucial situational option for Alston, and his timely contributions were vital in the Dodgers' pennant race and World Series run. Richert's ability to get out left-handed hitters proved invaluable in tight situations, becoming a reliable reliever for the team.

Dick Calmus (Born 1943, Debuted 1963): The Bonus Baby Arm.

Making his debut in 1963 at just 19 years old, Dick Calmus continued the Dodgers' tradition of bringing up incredibly young talent. Signed as a "bonus baby," Calmus was, by rule, required to remain on the big league roster for his first season, a challenging proposition for a teenager. In the 1963 championship season, he appeared in 21 games, primarily out of the bullpen, and posted a solid 3-1 record with a 2.66 ERA over 44.0 innings. His presence, though brief due to later arm troubles, underscored the depth of the Dodgers' pitching pipeline and their willingness to integrate youth directly into a contending team, even under restrictive rules.

The Foundation for a Dynasty

While the remaining Brooklyn veterans provided invaluable leadership and a strong core, it was the arrival and rapid development of these young players between 1958 and 1963 that truly solidified the Los Angeles Dodgers as a National League powerhouse. Players like Tommy Davis (a two-time batting champion and record-setting RBI man) and Willie Davis (the franchise's all-time stolen base leader and an unparalleled center fielder) injected consistent hitting and electrifying speed into the lineup. Frank Howard brought raw power that foreshadowed his 382 career home runs and became a fan favorite.

Crucially, this pivotal period also saw the full emergence of Sandy Koufax and Don Drysdale as two of the most dominant pitchers in baseball history, whose maturation into aces coincided perfectly with the arrival of these key position players. Drysdale's 25-win Cy Young season in 1962 and Koufax's increasingly unhittable performances set the stage for their unparalleled success. John Roseboro, who debuted just before the move, solidified his position as the team's durable, multi-time All-Star catcher, providing outstanding defense and expertly handling this formidable pitching staff.

These young men, many barely out of their teens, embraced the challenge of playing in a new city and on a new stage. They learned from their veteran teammates, adapted to the unique pressures of Los Angeles baseball and its distinct ballparks, and quickly became integral parts of a team that would go on to win World Series championships in 1959, 1963, and 1965. Their collective arrival and contributions during this pivotal period not only shaped the Dodgers' identity but also laid the groundwork for one of the most successful eras in the franchise's storied history, defined by elite pitching, fundamental defense, and electrifying speed.

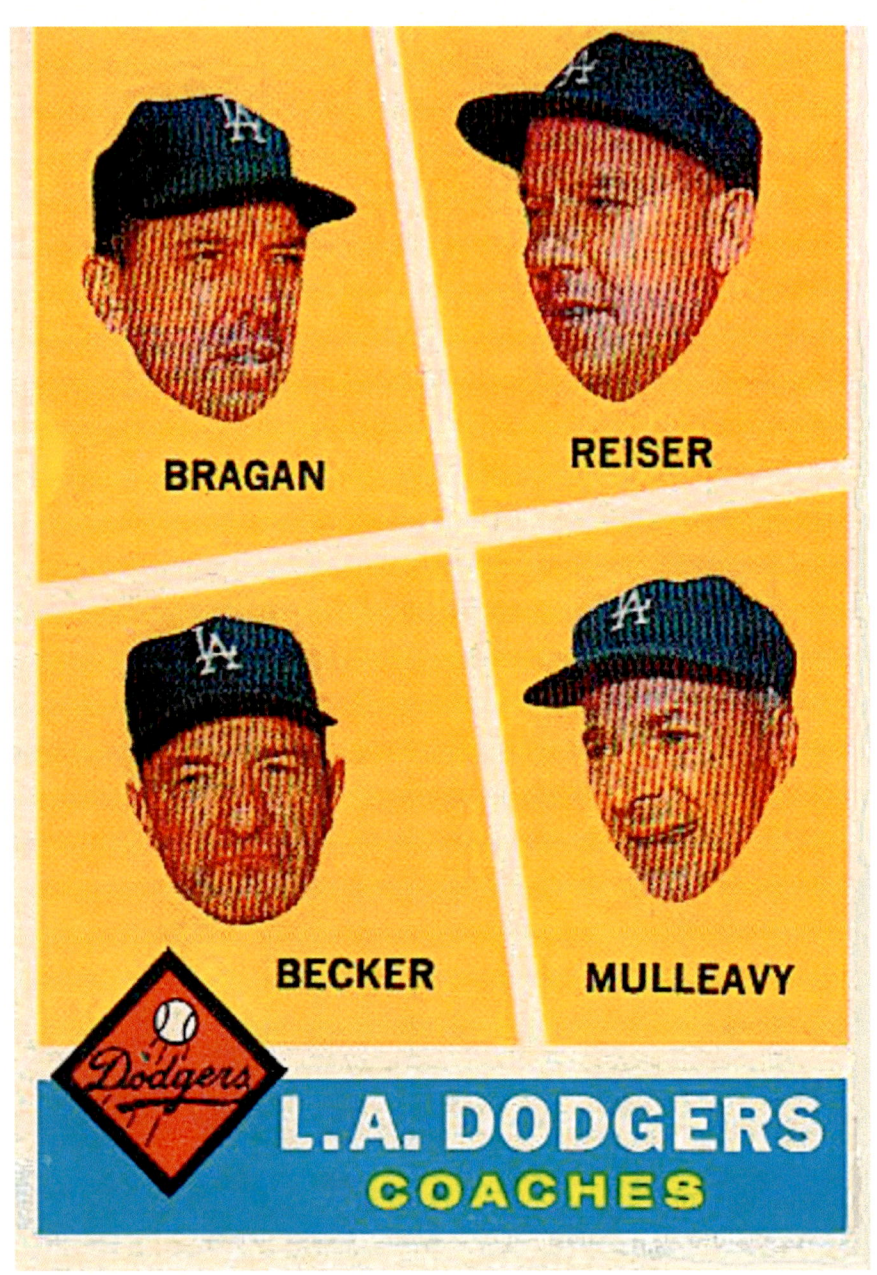

Dodger Coaches at the time.

1963 ROOKIE STARS

PEDRO GONZALEZ
N. Y. YANKEES, 2B

KEN McMULLEN
L. A. DODGERS, 3B

PETE ROSE
CINCINNATI REDS, 2B

AL WEIS
CHI. WHITE SOX, SS

Quirky Dodger Multi Player Rookie Card. One was sold at Auction for $717,000, not because Ken McMullen was on it but because it was Pete Rose's Rookie Card. This card is mint and has been in a protective plastic for over a half Century and was only removed for this scan from Author's Dodger Museum Collection.

Chapter Eleven
The Opening of Dodger Stadium and the heartbreak of 1962.

The 1962 Los Angeles Dodgers season stands as a monumental chapter in baseball history, a narrative woven with threads of grand ambition, statistical brilliance, and a dramatic, agonizing conclusion. This period marked a pivotal moment for the franchise as it sought to solidify its identity in Southern California, anchored by the unveiling of their magnificent new stadium. The season unfolded with immense anticipation, showcasing a talented roster and a fanbase eager for a championship in their new home. The events of 1962, from the celebratory opening of Dodger Stadium to the agonizing playoff series, encapsulate a story of soaring expectations and a profound, indelible disappointment. The Dodgers concluded the regular season with an impressive 101-61 record, a performance that underscored their potential and the high stakes involved as the season drew to a close. This record placed them in a dead heat with their fierce rivals, the San Francisco Giants, necessitating a best-of-three playoff series to determine the National League pennant winner. The team's exceptional performance throughout the regular season, leading to this decisive showdown, intrinsically heightened the pressure and public anticipation for a championship in their new venue. The relocation of the Dodgers from Brooklyn to Los Angeles in 1958 was a monumental undertaking, with the Los Angeles Memorial Coliseum serving as a temporary, albeit large, home for four seasons. The unveiling of Dodger Stadium in 1962 marked the culmination of years of complex planning, significant financial investment, and overcoming considerable local obstacles. As the first entirely privately financed major league stadium since Yankee Stadium in 1923, it symbolized a permanent and grand new chapter for the franchise in Southern California. The team's strong showing throughout the 1962 regular season, culminating in a tie for the pennant, amplified the pressure to deliver a championship in this state-of-the-art venue. It wasn't merely about winning a baseball title; it was about validating the controversial move, solidifying the team's identity in its new city, and fulfilling the promise of a truly "big league" experience for Los Angeles. Consequently, the eventual, dramatic collapse would feel even more devastating and indelible against this backdrop of immense civic pride and soaring hopes tied to their gleaming new home.

Below: Tapestry given to Walter O'Malley by Al Rabin "Peddler in Paradise" salesman which hung at O'Malley's office.

The grand opening of Dodger Stadium on April 10, 1962, was a landmark event, signaling the dawn of a new era for Major League Baseball in Southern California. Dodger Stadium was also the home ballpark for the American League's Los Angeles Angels in its inaugural year, a unique arrangement for a brand-new, privately financed venue. Gene Autry, owner of the Angels, publicly thanked Walter O'Malley for his attention to the beauty of the ballpark. The festivities commenced even before Opening Day with a special invitation-only dedication ceremony on April 9, 1962. This exclusive event, attended by sponsors, politicians, and key team executives, began with a celebratory parade from City Hall to the ballpark. Dignitaries such as Baseball Commissioner Ford C. Frick and National League President Warren Giles were present, with Commissioner Frick symbolically handing an oversized key to Dodger President Walter O'Malley, marking the official handover of the magnificent new facility. On April 10, 1962, the stadium was a complete sellout, a testament to the fervent anticipation surrounding its debut.

Fans, eager to experience the new ballpark, arrived early, with the gates opening at 10 a.m. to help manage traffic flow. The atmosphere was electric, enhanced by the sounds of Johnny Boudreau's band and Dodger organist Bob Mitchell, who entertained the early arrivals. For those unable to secure a ticket, the game was thoughtfully televised locally on KTTV Channel 11, ensuring widespread access to this historic occasion. The pre-game ceremonies were imbued with a sense of occasion. Renowned tenor Alma Pedroza delivered a stirring rendition of the national anthem at 12:45 p.m. At 1 p.m., Kay O'Malley, Walter O'Malley's wife, had the honor of throwing out the ceremonial first pitch from the seats behind the Dodger dugout to catcher John Roseboro, using a baseball autographed by the entire 1962 Dodger team. This gesture was a special "two-day early" birthday present from her husband.

April 10, 1962, Peter O'Malley looks on as his mother Kay gets ready to throw out the ceremonial first pitch from behind the Dodger dugout in the Field Level seats.

The inaugural game pitted the Dodgers against the Cincinnati Reds. At 1 p.m., Kay O'Malley, Walter O'Malley's wife, had the honor of throwing out the ceremonial first pitch from the seats behind the Dodger dugout to catcher John Roseboro, using a baseball autographed by the entire 1962 Dodger team. This gesture was a special "two-day early" birthday present from her husband. The inaugural game pitted the Dodgers against the Cincinnati Reds.

Johnny Podres, the hero of the Brooklyn Dodgers' World Series Championship in 1955, throws the first pitch in new Dodger Stadium.

Left-hander Johnny Podres, a celebrated hero from the Brooklyn Dodgers' 1955 World Series Championship, threw the stadium's historic first pitch. Hall of Fame umpire Al Barlick officiated behind the plate. Doug Harvey, also a Hall of Fame umpire, also made his major league debut at Dodger Stadium on April 10, 1962. Despite the celebratory atmosphere, the Reds spoiled the Dodgers' debut, securing a 6-3 victory. Eddie Kasko of the Reds recorded the first double, and Vada Pinson scored the first run in the new stadium. Duke Snider etched his name into history by registering the first hit for the Dodgers in their new home. The Dodgers would, however, earn their first victory at Dodger Stadium the following day, a 6-2 win powered by the pitching of Sandy Koufax. Walter O'Malley's vision for Dodger Stadium extended beyond its architectural grandeur; he oversaw every detail to ensure an unparalleled fan experience. The stadium was renowned for its immaculate cleanliness, featuring sparkling concrete floors and an impressive 48 well-maintained restrooms, exceeding that of any other ballpark at the time. Concession stands were spacious and easily accessible, contributing to an overall environment that was family-friendly, comfortable, and safe, where the game remained the central attraction. The extensive landscaping, including iconic swaying palm trees and vibrant flowers, enhanced the stadium's first-class image. A time capsule containing significant memorabilia such as sports pages, yearbooks, programs, and official documents from the opening days was also placed within the stadium, symbolizing its enduring legacy. Among the notable figures present on Opening Day, beyond the O'Malley's, Commissioner Frick, and President Giles, were key Dodgers players who formed the inaugural lineup. These included Maury Wills at shortstop, Jim Gilliam at second base, Wally Moon in left field, Duke Snider in right field, John Roseboro behind the plate, Ron Fairly at first base, Daryl Spencer at third base, Willie Davis in center field, and Johnny Podres as the starting pitcher. Manager Walter Alston was also featured, ready to lead his team into this new era.

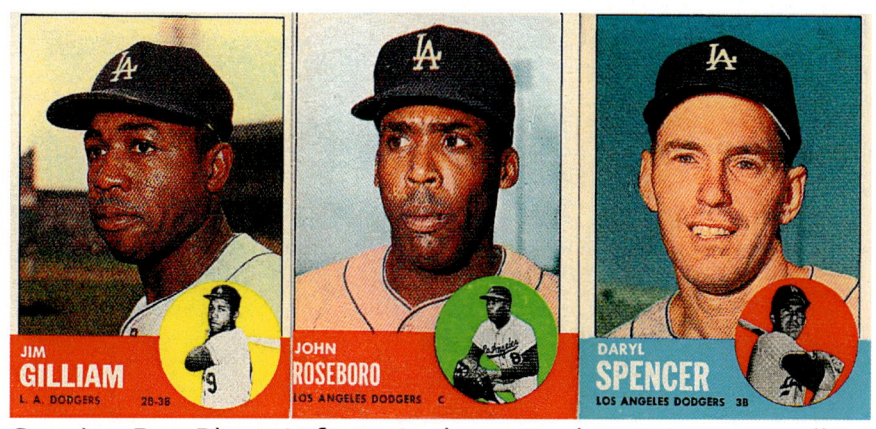

Starting Day Player's from Author's Dodger Museum Collection.

The detailed accounts from Walter O'Malley's official website consistently highlight his unwavering commitment to creating a state-of-the-art, fan-centric ballpark. Within this narrative of grand achievement, the anecdote about "O'Malley's Oasis"—the initial oversight of only two drinking fountains in the dugouts on Opening Day—serves as a fascinating, humanizing detail. While seemingly minor, this detail illustrates the immense logistical complexities of constructing such a massive venue under tight deadlines. The swift resolution of this issue and the overall emphasis on cleanliness, abundant restrooms, and family-friendly amenities reinforce O'Malley's dedication to the fan experience. This small "hiccup" paradoxically strengthens the perception of his meticulousness and responsiveness, demonstrating that even in a monumental undertaking, the details mattered, and any shortcomings were quickly addressed to maintain the stadium's first-class image.

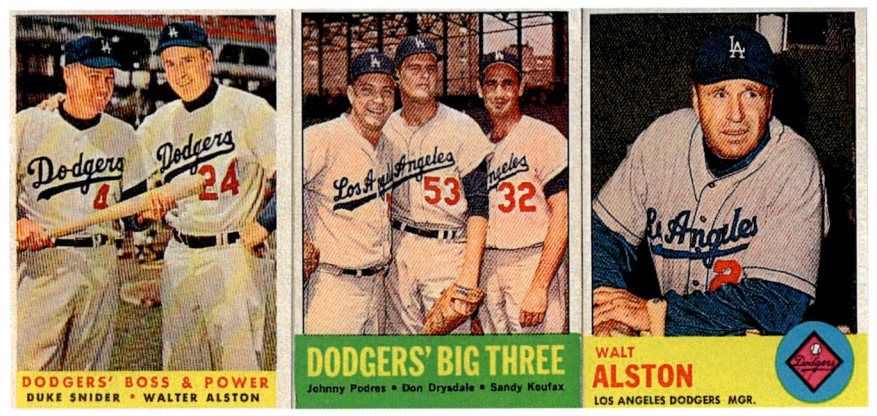

Cards from Author's Dodger Museum Collection.

The Los Angeles Dodgers' 1962 season was characterized by impressive statistical performance across batting and pitching. The team concluded the regular season with 101 wins and 61 losses, achieving a .623 winning percentage, which then led to a tie-breaking playoff for the pennant. Their home record was powerful at 54-27, complemented by a solid 47-34 record on the road. The Dodgers' offense was a formidable force throughout the 162-game 1962 campaign. The team accumulated 5,628 at-bats, scored 842 runs, and recorded 1,510 hits. Their collective batting average was .268, ranking them 4th in the league. A distinctive feature of their offensive strategy was their league-leading 65 triples, an impressive 198 stolen bases (also leading the league), and a league-best .337 on-base percentage. They ranked

2nd in runs scored and 3rd in RBIs, showcasing their ability to generate offense consistently. The team's league-best on-base percentage (OBP) was .337, while their slugging percentage (SLG) was .400, ranking eighth. Despite their offensive prowess, they hit 140 home runs, placing them 7th in the league. The Dodgers' pitching staff also delivered a strong performance, contributing to their 101 wins against 61 losses (regular season), tying for 1st in the league for wins. Their team Earned Run Average (ERA) was 3.62, placing them 3rd in the league. The pitching staff led the league in strikeouts with 1,104 and topped the league in innings pitched with 1488.2. Additionally, they ranked 2nd in saves with 44. They allowed 1,386 hits and 598 earned runs, ranking 4th in the NL for both categories. An in-depth review of the Dodgers' 1962 team batting statistics reveals a striking characteristic of their offensive approach: despite ranking highly in runs scored and RBIs, they were notably lower in home runs yet led the entire National League in triples and stolen bases. This statistical pattern indicates a deliberate and highly effective offensive philosophy that diverged from the power-hitting strategies often associated with successful teams. Their high run production was achieved not through the "long ball" but through manufacturing runs via aggressive baserunning, hitting for contact, and extra-base hits that didn't clear the fence. This approach would have placed immense pressure on opposing defenses and pitchers, compelling them to execute flawlessly to prevent runs from being scored by players advancing on singles or taking extra bases. It highlights how the Dodgers' offensive identity was deeply rooted in speed and fundamental baseball. This strategic choice defined their success in an era preceding the full embrace of home run-centric offenses.

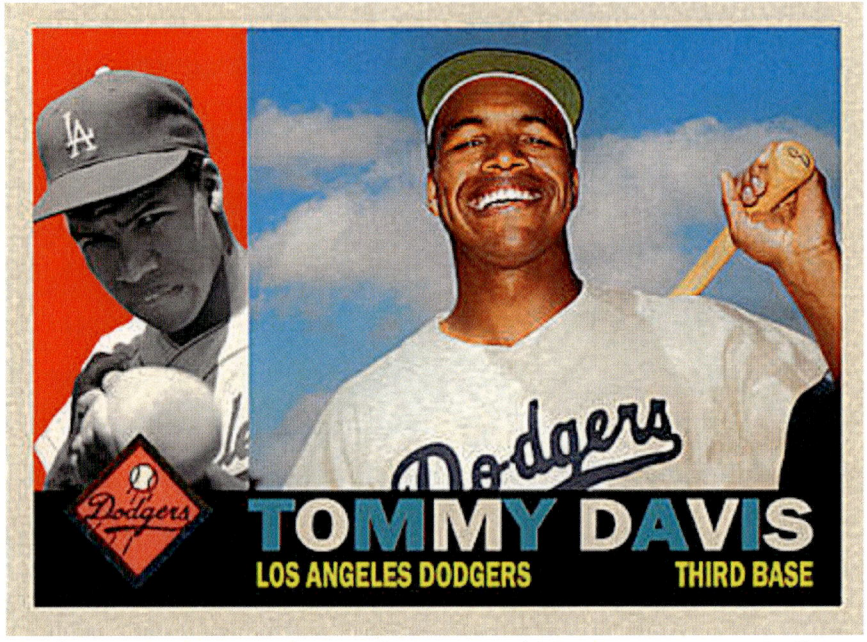

Dodger "Hitting Machine" from Brooklyn, Tommy Davis from Authors' Dodger Museum Collection.

The 1962 Los Angeles Dodgers featured several individual stars who distinguished themselves among the National League's elite, contributing significantly to the team's impressive season. Tommy Davis had an extraordinary year, leading the National League in multiple key offensive categories. He finished first in batting average (.346), hits (230), and RBIs (153). Beyond these league-leading marks, he also contributed 27 doubles and 27 home runs and scored 120 runs. His 153 RBIs set a new Dodgers franchise record, surpassing Roy Campanella's mark, and remains the highest in franchise history. Davis was only the seventh player in National League history to drive 150 runs in a single season. Maury Wills was recognized for his exceptional performance by winning the National League MVP award. Playing in all 165 games (including playoffs), he recorded 695 at-bats and 208 hits, maintaining a batting average of .299. His most remarkable achievement was leading the league in stolen bases with an astounding 104, a feat that showcased his game-changing speed. He also scored 130 runs, demonstrating his ability to get on base and create scoring opportunities. On the pitching mound, Don Drysdale was the team's undisputed ace. He led the National League in games started (41), innings pitched (314.1), and wins (25). His impressive ERA of 2.83 further solidified his dominance. Drysdale's stellar season was recognized with the Cy Young Award in 1962, which at the time was awarded to the best pitcher in all of Major League Baseball.

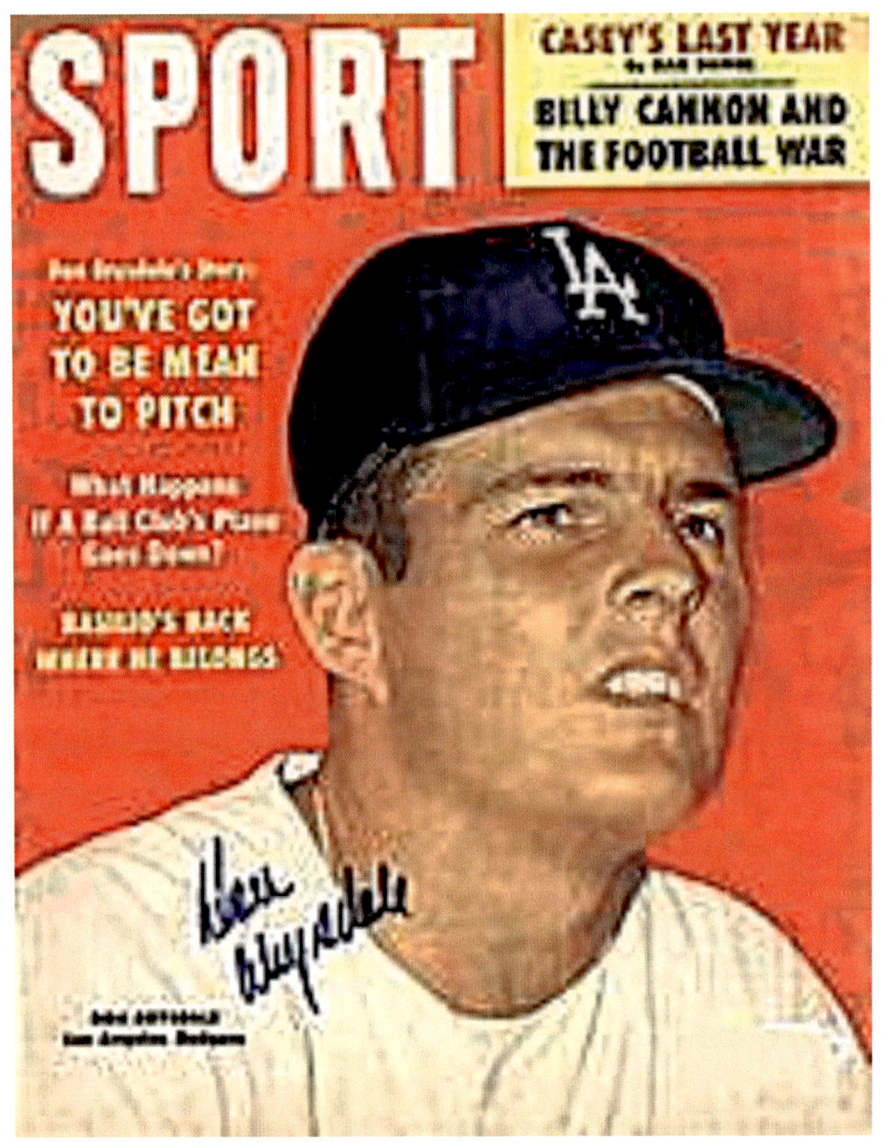

Autographed Magazine Cover from Author's Dodger Museum Collection.

Despite battling a serious finger injury that impacted his starts after July 12, Sandy Koufax still managed to post remarkable numbers. He led the league with an exceptional ERA of 2.54 and a league-best 10.546 strikeouts per 9 innings. He concluded the season with 14 wins and seven losses, good for a .667 win-loss percentage. Koufax also led the league in hits per 9 innings (6.542) and Walks and Hits per Inning Pitched (1.036), indicating his elite control and ability to limit baserunners. Regarding power, Frank Howard significantly contributed to the Dodgers' offense, hitting 31 home runs and driving in 119 RBIs. His slugging percentage of .560 highlighted his ability to hit for extra bases. The Dodgers' bullpen relied heavily on key relievers. Ron Perranoski led the entire National League in games played with 70 appearances and ranked 2nd in saves with 19. Ed Roebuck was another frequently used reliever, appearing in 64 games. Larry Sherry also played a critical role, pitching in 58 games and recording 11 saves. While the brilliance of Don Drysdale and Sandy Koufax is undeniable and well-documented, a closer examination of the pitching data reveals a critical underlying dynamic: the immense workload shouldered by the Dodgers' top relievers. Ron Perranoski led the entire league in games played, and Ed Roebuck was third, indicating a heavy reliance on a minimal core of bullpen arms. This reliance, coupled with Drysdale and Johnny Podres being among the league leaders in games started and innings pitched, paints a picture of a pitching staff built on the backs of a few workhorses. While effective for much of the season, this intense usage inherently created a vulnerability to fatigue and injury for these key pitchers as the season progressed into the high-pressure tie-breaker series.

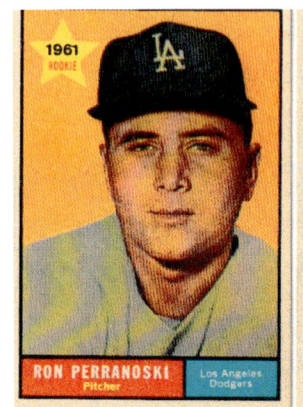

The bulk of the Dodgers saves came from these three relievers.

It foreshadows the later discussion of Walter Alston's controversial decisions, as bullpen management and pitcher availability became critical factors in the season's outcome.

The 1962 National League pennant race culminated in one of baseball's most dramatic finishes: a test of endurance and nerve. Both the Los Angeles Dodgers and the San Francisco Giants concluded the grueling 162-game regular season with identical 101-61 records, an outcome that necessitated a best-of-three tie-breaker series to determine the league champion. It marked only the fifth time in Major League Baseball history that a regular season playoff was required. The rivalry between these two franchises, deeply rooted in their shared New York origins before moving to California, was already intense, and the high-stakes playoff only amplified its ferocity. Game 1 of the series occurred on October 1, 1962, at Candlestick Park in San Francisco. The Giants delivered a dominant performance, shutting out the Dodgers 8-0. Dodgers manager Walter Alston's decision to start Sandy Koufax proved a gamble that didn't pay off. Koufax was still recovering from a serious finger injury that had significantly hampered his effectiveness since July 12. He lasted only one inning, surrendering four hits and three runs, setting a difficult tone for the Dodgers from the outset. The Giants' offense, meanwhile, was powered by home runs from Orlando Cepeda, Jim Davenport, and two from the legendary Willie Mays. Giants' pitcher Billy Pierce delivered a masterful performance, throwing a three-hit shutout. The game was also marked by controversy regarding the field conditions. Giants' manager Alvin Dark reportedly ordered the Candlestick Park grounds crew to soak the base paths, a tactic aimed at slowing down the Dodgers' speed demon, Maury Wills. This wasn't the first instance of alleged groundskeeping interference; similar tactics, including "harrowing" and excessive watering, had been reported in prior Giants-Dodgers series at Candlestick Park earlier that season. Although umpire Jocko Conlan ordered the field repaired, it remained mushy. Maury Wills later stated that the muddy conditions demoralized the team and negatively affected their hitting, suggesting a tangible impact beyond physical impediment. Game 2, played on October 2, 1962, at Dodger Stadium, saw a dramatic shift in momentum. Facing elimination, the

Dodgers mounted a remarkable comeback. Trailing 5-0 in the seventh inning, the Dodgers' offense exploded for seven runs, breaking a frustrating 35-inning scoreless streak. They ultimately secured an 8-7 victory with a decisive run in the bottom of the ninth inning. This thrilling contest was, at the time, a very long nine-inning game in MLB history. Maury Wills played a heroic role in the Game 2 victory, scoring the winning run after hitting a ball up the middle that resulted in a single and an error, allowing him to reach second base. Stan Williams earned the win for the Dodgers in relief. The Giants' deliberate act of soaking the base paths at Candlestick Park before Game 1 transcends simple gamesmanship; it represents a calculated act of psychological warfare aimed directly at Maury Wills, the Dodgers' speed demon and MVP. It wasn't merely a minor inconvenience; Wills's direct statement about the mud "demoralizing" the team and affecting their hitting establishes a causal link between this external, seemingly minor manipulation of playing conditions and the team's mental state and on-field performance. It suggests that the Giants understood the Dodgers' reliance on speed and sought to undermine it physically and psychologically. The fact that the Dodgers were "really demoralized" and "could not concentrate properly at the plate" indicates that this tactic had a tangible, negative impact beyond just slowing Wills down. It set a tense, emotionally charged backdrop for the decisive Game 3, where every decision and every perceived slight would be magnified.

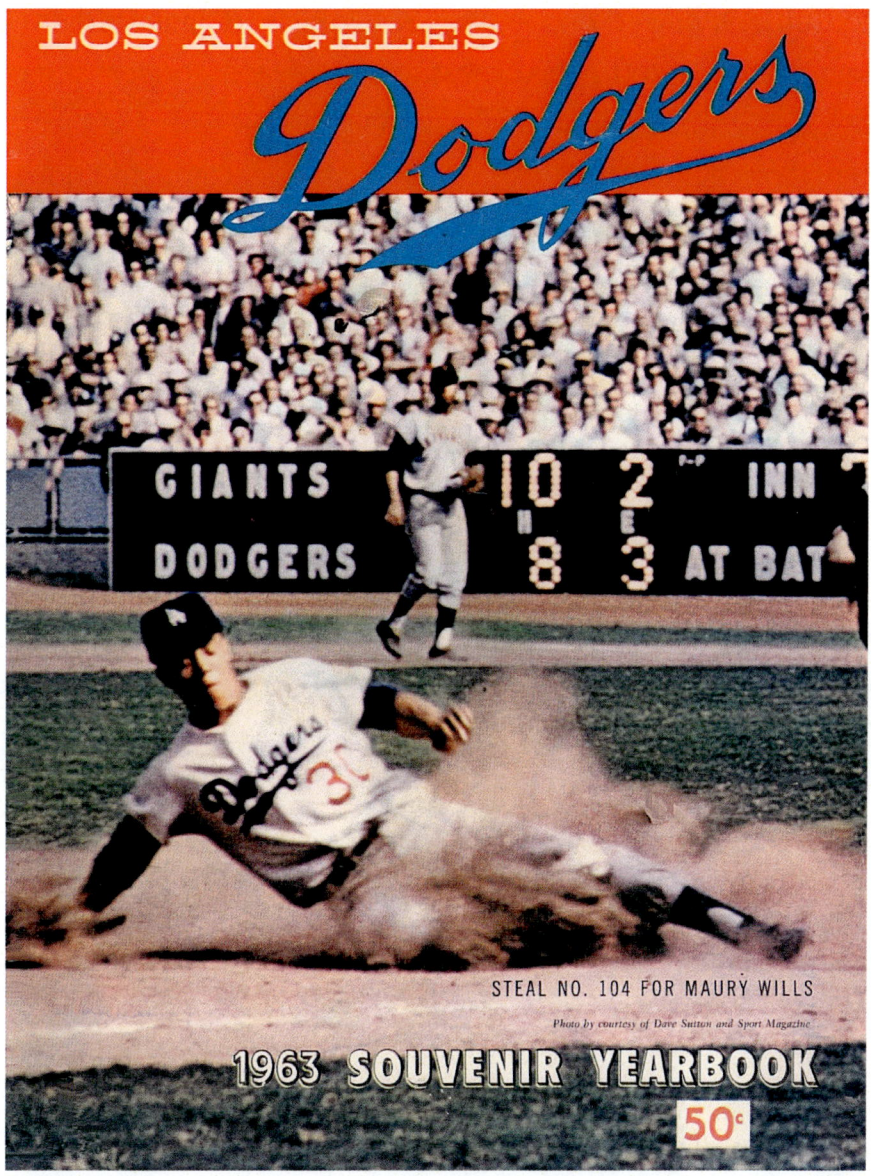

Maury Wills record steal # 104 against Giants in the playoffs from 1963 Yearbook in Author's Dodger Museum Collection.

ALLEN SCHERY

The fate of the 1962 National League pennant came down to Game 3, played on October 3, 1962, at Dodger Stadium. In a dramatic and heartbreaking contest for Dodgers fans, the San Francisco Giants emerged victorious with a 6-4 win, clinching the pennant. This decisive game became infamous for a series of controversial managerial decisions made by Dodgers manager Walter Alston, which have been debated and analyzed for decades. Several contextual factors contributed to the challenging circumstances Alston faced in Game 3. Sandy Koufax, one of the Dodgers' ace pitchers, was recovering from a serious finger injury that had significantly affected his performance and reliability since July. This injury meant he wasn't a viable option for extended relief, placing additional strain on an already taxed bullpen. The Dodgers' primary relievers, Ron Perranoski, Ed Roebuck, and Larry Sherry, had collectively pitched over three hundred relief innings throughout the season, suggesting a significant level of fatigue as the season reached its climax. Some observers have posited that if these key relievers had been better rested at the end of the season, the Dodgers might have secured the pennant. Furthermore, Don Drysdale, the team's other dominant starter, had thrown a strenuous 102 pitches just twenty-four hours earlier in Game 2, making him a less viable option for immediate or extended relief in the decisive Game 3. These limitations severely constrained Alston's top pitching options when the game was on the line. The game's turning points were marked by a series of critical moves by Alston, which have been meticulously scrutinized. The most infamous came in the top of the ninth inning, with the Dodgers holding a 4-2 lead. Alston left a struggling Ed Roebuck in to pitch, despite his coach Leo Durocher's reported urging to make a change. Roebuck issued a walk to Felipe Alou, then allowed a single to Willie Mays. Orlando Cepeda followed with another single, scoring Alou and cutting the lead to 4-3, at which point Alston finally brought in Stan Williams. Williams then gave up a groundout to Jim Davenport that scored Mays, tying the game at 4-4. After an intentional walk to Ed Bailey and a single by Manny Mota, Alston turned to Ron Perranoski, who then yielded a grounder to Jose Pagan, which second baseman Larry Burright committed an error on, allowing another run to score and extend the Giants' lead to 6-4. In the bottom of the 9th, Billy Pierce came in to pitch for the Giants and closed the game with a perfect ninth inning, retiring Maury Wills, Jim Gilliam, and Lee Walls in order. The Giants scored four runs in the top of the ninth inning to erase a two-run deficit and take a 6-4 lead, ultimately holding the Dodgers scoreless in the bottom of the 9th to win the game and clinch the 1962 National League Pennant, sending them to the World Series against the New York Yankees. Player and coach perspectives from the game reveal a sense of bewilderment. Coach Leo Durocher's assessment that Roebuck was "done" directly challenged Alston's decision-making. Other players, including Duke Snider, Maury Wills, Ron Fairly, Larry Sherry,

John Roseboro, and Stan Williams, also offered their views on these questionable moves, with a general sentiment of confusion regarding Williams's continued presence and Drysdale's absence. While these decisions drew heavy criticism, it's also important to consider that some of Alston's moves were "somewhat defensible." For instance, the decision not to use Drysdale was partly due to his high pitch count from the previous day's game. Furthermore, Alston's reliance on a few key relievers like Perranoski earlier in the season stemmed from a lack of trust in other organizational pitchers for mop-up duties, which inadvertently contributed to the bullpen's overall fatigue by the season's end. The detailed enumeration of Walter Alston's critical decisions in Game 3 reveals more than just isolated tactical errors; it exposes a cascading series of choices that, when viewed collectively, created a chain of events leading to the Dodgers' collapse. The core issue stems from a season-long over-reliance on a limited number of key relievers, which led to their significant fatigue by the season's end. This fatigue, coupled with Sandy Koufax's finger injury rendering him unreliable after July and Don Drysdale's high pitch count from the previous day, severely constrained Alston's available, fresh, and effective pitching options. The repeated instances of not replacing a struggling pitcher aren't just poor in-game calls; they are symptoms of a manager operating within severe limitations, misjudging the immediate effectiveness of his fatigued pitchers, or genuinely having no better, rested alternatives. This sequence of events highlights how long-term roster management and pitching usage throughout a grueling season can directly lead to critical failures when the stakes are highest, transforming seemingly minor decisions into catastrophic ones. While the 1962 collapse is often attributed to Walter Alston's "bad decisions," a deeper analysis reveals these were complex, potentially defensible choices made under extreme pressure and severe pitching limitations. The research indicates that "all of these moves were at least somewhat defensible." It acknowledges Alston's extensive track record of success, having "won many games over the years." The fact that legendary broadcaster Vin Scully, known for his professionalism, didn't point fingers at Alston's decisions during the live broadcast suggests that in the heat of the moment, these choices might not have appeared as egregious or wrong as they did in hindsight, particularly given the limited information and options available to Alston. This perspective shifts the analysis from merely labeling decisions as "good" or "bad" to understanding the immense pressure, the real-time constraints, and the subjective nature of managerial calls in high-stakes environments. It implies that Alston was making the best choices he believed he had, even if they ultimately didn't yield the desired outcome, rather than simply making irrational errors. The immediate fallout from the 1962 collapse was a torrent of frustration from Dodgers fans, leading to "many calls for Alston's head on a platter."

ALLEN SCHERY

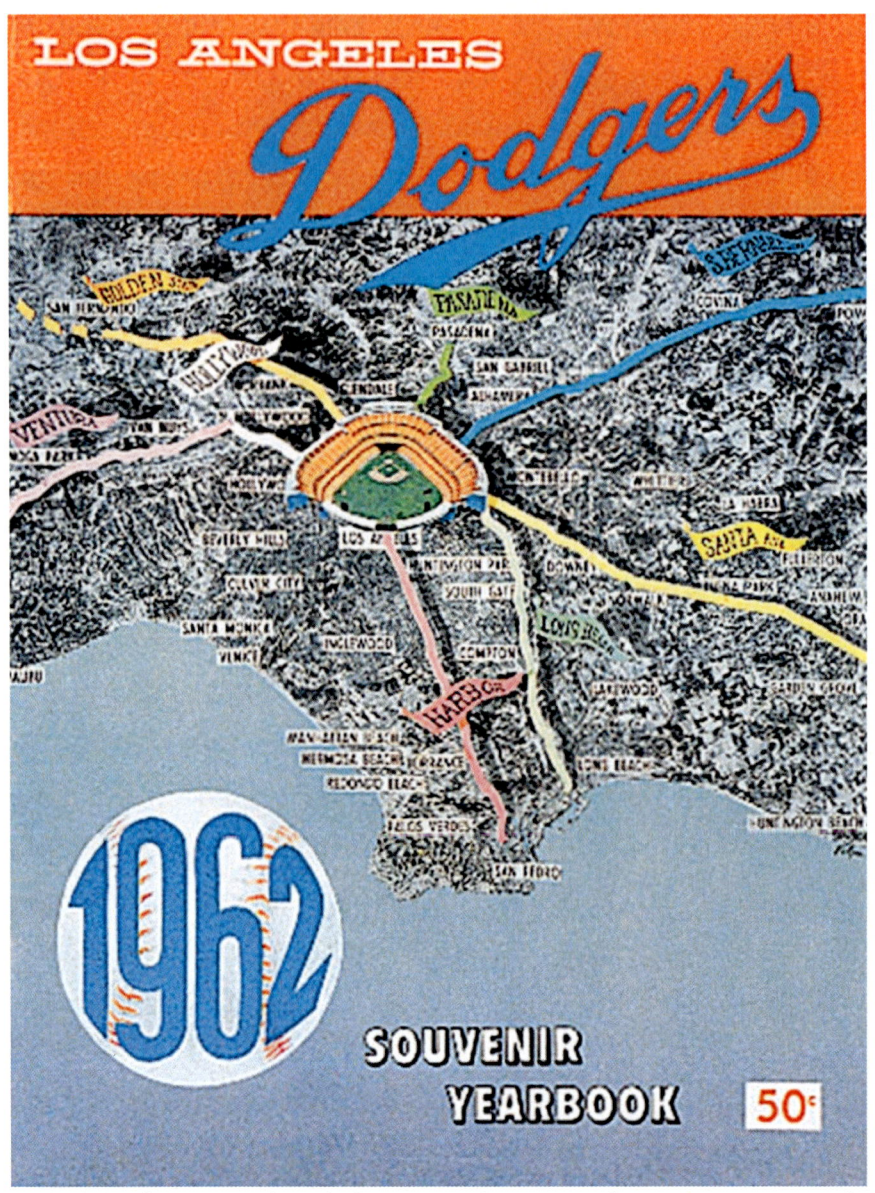

1962 Dodger Yearbook from Author's Dodger Museum Collection.

The 1962 team largely remained intact for the subsequent seasons. A significant change in the pitching staff's dynamics contributed to future success: Sandy Koufax and Don Drysdale, the team's two ace starters, would consistently pitch deep into games, with both individually exceeding 300 innings pitched in key subsequent seasons, significantly reducing the strain on the bullpen. This shift suggests that the increased durability and workload of the starting rotation effectively mitigated the bullpen fatigue issues experienced in 1962. The Dodgers' resilience was quickly evident. Following the 1962 disappointment, the team achieved remarkable success, winning the National League pennant in 1963, 1965, and 1966 and securing two World Series championships. This rapid and sustained return to dominance demonstrated the strength of the team's core and the enduring effectiveness of Alston's leadership. From a historical perspective, Walter Alston has essentially been "forgiven" for the 1962 loss, especially when viewed against the backdrop of the Dodgers' four pennants in that era (1959, 1963, 1965, 1966) and three World Series titles. The intense self-flagellation often seen in other fan bases after similar collapses, such as Red Sox fans in 1978 or 2003, wasn't as pronounced for the 1962 Dodgers, likely due to their swift and impressive return to championship contention. The most profound observation from the aftermath of the 1962 season is the Dodgers' front office's decision to retain Walter Alston despite widespread public outrage and calls for his dismissal.

It wasn't a passive choice. The rumor that Walter O'Malley considered firing Alston, only for General Manager Buzzie Bavasi to reportedly threaten resignation in protest, highlights a deep, almost counter-intuitive, organizational trust in Alston's long-term capabilities. Bavasi's argument that Alston wasn't "the guy who threw the pitches, swung the bat, etc." indicates an understanding that the loss wasn't solely attributable to managerial decisions but perhaps to broader team issues or unavoidable circumstances, such as injuries and fatigue. The subsequent rapid success of the Dodgers, winning three more pennants and two World Series titles in the next four years, serves as a robust validation of this organizational stability and trust. It demonstrates a crucial management principle: sometimes, unwavering belief in a proven leader, even after a significant public setback, can foster resilience and yield greater long-term success than a reactive, emotionally driven change. The research explicitly draws a direct causal line between the health and workload of the Dodgers' starting pitchers and the performance of their bullpen. Significantly, it then states that in the subsequent, successful years (1963, 1965, 1966), with Koufax and Drysdale both pitching over 300 innings, "the bullpen got better. Mainly because Alston did not have to use it as much." It establishes a clear cause-and-effect relationship: a healthy, dominant starting rotation that consistently goes deep into games directly reduces the strain and fatigue on the bullpen, thereby improving its overall effectiveness.

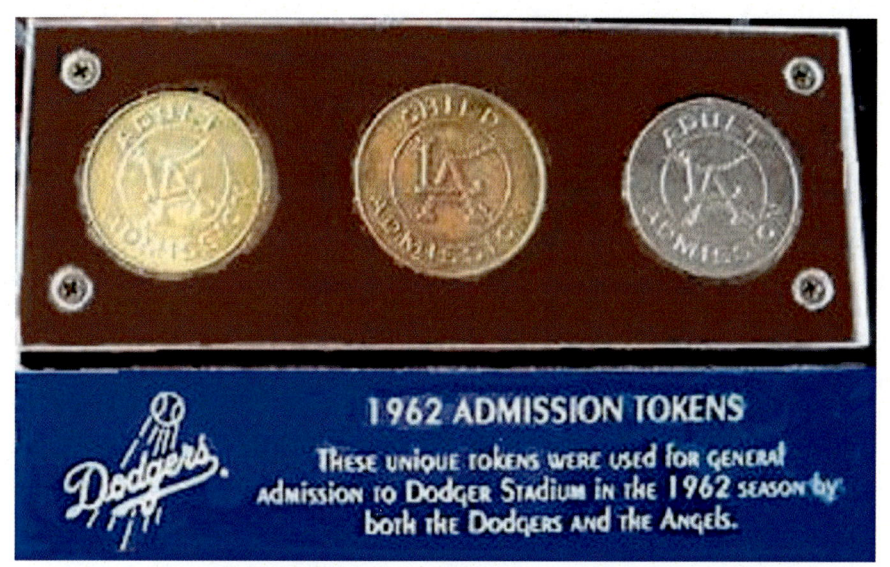

Tokens used at Dodger Stadium in 1962 from Author's Dodger Museum Collection.

The 1962 collapse, in this light, wasn't just about Alston's in-game decisions but a symptom of a deeper, systemic issue of an overtaxed bullpen due to an injured ace. The subsequent success directly resulted from the starting pitchers carrying their intended load, alleviating pressure on the relievers. The 1962 Los Angeles Dodgers season represents a complex tapestry of triumph and tribulation. It began with the historic inauguration of Dodger Stadium. This privately funded marvel symbolized the franchise's permanent establishment in Southern California and Walter O'Malley's determined vision for the future of baseball. This new home, shared with the American League's Los Angeles Angels, and a roster boasting league leaders like Tommy Davis and MVP Maury Wills fueled immense expectations for a championship. The team's statistical dominance in 1962, particularly their unique blend of speed and contact hitting, underscored their potential. While Walter Alston's game three managerial choices were heavily criticized, a comprehensive analysis reveals they were made under extreme pressure and within the constraints of an overtaxed bullpen and injured starting pitchers. The season's outcome highlighted the critical interdependence of a healthy, durable starting rotation and a rested, effective bullpen. Despite the bitter disappointment of 1962, the Dodgers' organizational stability and the front office's trust in Walter Alston proved to be a strategic masterstroke, as the day after losing the National League Pennant, the organization internally declared, "the 1963 season begins now." The decision to retain Alston, even amidst public outcry, allowed the team's core to mature and for the pitching staff to regain its full strength. This stability directly contributed to the Dodgers' rapid return to prominence, culminating in multiple pennants and World Series titles in the years immediately following the 1962 collapse. Ultimately, the 1962 season, with its blend of grand openings, individual brilliance, and a dramatic downfall, served as a foundational, albeit painful, learning experience that paved the way for a golden era of Dodgers baseball. The lessons learned and the resilience forged in 1962 set the stage for the Dodgers' glorious run to the World Series championship in 1963.

EBBETS TO PARADISE-O'MALLEY'S JOURNEY TO THE COLISEUM &...

These were the first 2 1/2" Pins sold at Dodger Stadium from the Author's Dodger Museum Collection.

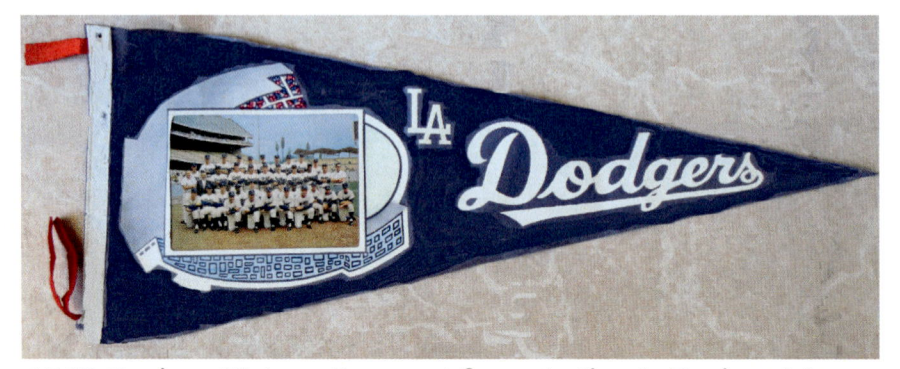

1962 Dodger Picture Pennant from Author's Dodger Museum Collection.

Chapter Twelve

The Unforgettable Sweep: How the 1963 Dodgers Conquered the Yankees

The 1963 Los Angeles Dodgers achieved a season of redemption and triumph, which culminated in a historic four-game sweep of the formidable New York Yankees in the World Series. After finishing the regular season with a dominant 99-63 record to secure the National League pennant by a comfortable six-game margin, the Dodgers featured an unparalleled pitching staff and a potent offense. Led by the exceptional Sandy Koufax, who earned both the National League MVP and World Series MVP awards, alongside pitching ace Don Drysdale and offensive stars like Tommy Davis and Maury Wills, the team delivered a lesson in efficiency. Their pitching stifled the Yankees' potent lineup, holding them to just four runs across the entire series. This marked the first time in history that the perennial American League champions were swept in a World Series, signaling a definitive changing of the guard in Major League Baseball.

The 1963 National League Season: A Summary

The 1963 Los Angeles Dodgers' National League season was a resounding success, marked by strong pitching, timely hitting, and a dramatic pennant race that ultimately saw them emerge victorious. Coming off a disappointing 1962 season that ended in a tie-breaker loss, the Dodgers rebounded with a dominant 99-63 record, securing the National League pennant by a six-game margin over the St. Louis Cardinals. The team's success was anchored mainly by its exceptional pitching staff, which led the league with a 2.85 ERA and a club-record 24 shutouts. At the forefront was Sandy Koufax, who had a career year, winning both the National League MVP and Cy Young Award (the first unanimous choice). Despite early career struggles with control and a circulatory problem in his left hand that had sidelined him in 1962, Koufax transformed into a dominant force, posting a remarkable 25-5 record with an astonishing 1.88 ERA and 11 shutouts, becoming the first modern NL pitcher to surpass 300 strikeouts (finishing with 306). He also threw his second career no-hitter in May. While Koufax was the ace, the entire rotation was strong. Don Drysdale, though not matching his incredible 1962 win total, still contributed significantly with a 19-17 record over 315 innings. His imposing presence and heavy workload were crucial to the staff's success, even as he often battled for run support.

TURN BACK THE CLOCK: 1963

SANDY KOUFAX DOMINATES SEASON

In 1963 Sandy Koufax swept the Awards

Ace reliever Ron Perranoski was also a key factor, boasting a 16-3 record with 21 saves and a 1.67 ERA in 69 appearances.

Offensively, the Dodgers were led by Tommy Davis, who captured his second consecutive NL batting title with a .326 average and drove in 88 runs. Maury Wills, the reigning NL MVP from 1962, continued to be a dynamic force on the basepaths, hitting .302 and swiping 40 bases, while also showcasing his dazzling defensive prowess at shortstop. Frank Howard provided power, leading the team with 28 home runs. Beyond these stars, the offense relied on timely hitting and strategic baserunning, with contributions from steady players like Jim Gilliam and John Roseboro, who also provided crucial defensive stability behind the plate.

Three of the World Champs key players from Author's Dodger Museum Collection.

The pennant race was not without its challenges. The St. Louis Cardinals mounted a fierce charge in September, winning 19 of 20 games to close within one game of the Dodgers. However, Los Angeles showed remarkable resilience, winning a crucial three-game series in St. Louis in mid-September, including a pivotal 1-0 shutout victory, to re-establish their lead and clinch the pennant before the season's final day.

The 1963 National League season demonstrated the Dodgers' growth and maturation, particularly their ability to overcome past setbacks and harness their immense talent into a cohesive championship-caliber team. Manager Walter Alston, known for his calm demeanor and ability to extract consistent performance from his players, expertly guided this transformation, fostering a culture of resilience and disciplined play.

A Season of Redemption and Transformation The 1963 season was a profound narrative of redemption for the Dodgers following the significant disappointment of 1962. That year, the state-of-the-art Dodger Stadium, a symbol of a new era for baseball in Los Angeles, opened its gates on April 10, 1962. While a monumental architectural achievement, the stadium's debut did not immediately translate into on-field success, leaving the promise of a "new era" unfulfilled for a year. However, the 1963 World Series victory fundamentally reshaped the stadium's symbolic meaning. Clinching the championship at Dodger Stadium transformed it from merely an impressive new venue into a hallowed ground where a championship was won, fulfilling the vision of that "new era" and cementing its place in baseball lore as a home of champions, not just a site of past disappointments. The triumph also ignited immense excitement among the Los Angeles fanbase, solidifying the Dodgers' place in the city's sporting identity.

The Los Angeles Dodgers rebounded emphatically in 1963, demonstrating significant improvement and consistency throughout the regular season. Exceptional individual performances powered the team's success. Sandy Koufax's excellence was a continuation of his 1962 season, where he led the NL in several key pitching categories, including Earned Run Average (2.54), Walks and Hits per Inning Pitched (1.036), Hits per 9 Innings (6.542), and Strikeouts per 9 Innings (10.546), accumulating 216 strikeouts overall.

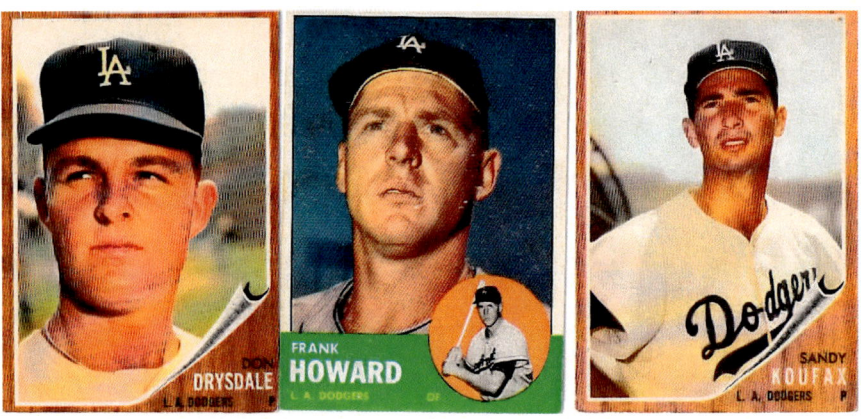

Three of the Major Stars from 1963 World Series sweep of the Yankees from Author's Dodger Museum Collection.

His salary reflected his growing value, increasing from $27,500 in 1962 to $35,000 in 1963. Tommy Davis continued his stellar hitting from the previous year. In 1962, he led the National League in batting average (.346), hits (230), and RBIs (153), establishing new Dodgers franchise records. Don Drysdale, another pitching ace, was instrumental, leading the NL in wins (25) and innings pitched (314.1) in 1962, maintaining a strong 2.83 ERA. Maury Wills, the NL MVP in 1962, set a team record with 104 stolen bases and 208 hits. Frank Howard led the team with 31 home runs and 119 RBIs in 1962. Tommy Davis led the team with 153 RBIs in 1962. The 1963 Dodgers' strong regular season performance and individual player accolades were not simply a sudden emergence of talent. Instead, they represented the maturation of a highly skilled roster that had endured the painful lessons of the 1962 season. The organizational decision to maintain the team's core, despite public pressure for managerial changes, proved pivotal. This continuity allowed the players to build upon their collective experience, transforming the previous year's near-miss into a catalyst for growth and refinement. For instance, criticisms regarding bullpen over-reliance in 1962 led to a more strategic deployment of pitchers in 1963, resulting in a more rested and effective relief corps. This strategic adjustment, born directly from the challenges of 1962, contributed significantly to the overall stability and success of the team, demonstrating a direct connection between past adversity and future triumph.

The World Series Showdown The 1963 World Series presented a classic matchup, pitting the Los Angeles Dodgers against the New York Yankees, a franchise that had long dominated the American League and held a storied rivalry with the Dodgers dating back to their Brooklyn days. The Yankees entered the series as two-time defending World Series champions, claiming titles in 1961 and 1962. Their sustained excellence was evident in their 1963 regular season performance, where they finished with an impressive 104-57 record, securing their 28th pennant and winning the American League by a commanding 10.5 games over the Chicago White Sox. While still formidable, an aging core and increasing injury concerns for key players like Mickey Mantle and Roger Maris hinted at a potential shift in their dynastic reign. The Yankees' formidable roster boasted a lineup filled with established stars and powerful hitters: Elston Howard, the American League MVP in 1963, hit .287 with 28 home runs and 85 RBIs. Joe Pepitone contributed significantly with 27 home runs and 89 RBIs. Despite being limited to just 90 games due to injuries, Roger Maris still managed to hit 23 home runs and 53 RBIs. Even with a shortened season of 65 games, Mickey Mantle remained dangerous, batting .314 with 15 home runs and 35 RBIs. Their pitching staff was equally impressive, featuring future Hall of Famer Whitey Ford, who posted a 24-7 record with a 2.74 ERA and 189 strikeouts. Ralph Terry contributed 17 wins and a 3.22 ERA, while Jim Bouton added 21 wins and a 2.53 ERA. This combination of offensive firepower and top-tier pitching made the Yankees a perennial powerhouse. The historical context of the Yankees' dominance significantly elevates the achievement of the 1963 Dodgers' sweep. The Yankees were not merely a strong team but a long-standing dynasty that had consistently reigned over Major League Baseball for decades. The Dodgers' four-game sweep transcends a typical championship victory by emphasizing their status as two-time defending champions and their impressive 1963 regular season record. It became a symbolic "changing of the guard" in Major League Baseball, a decisive dethroning of a titan. This historical backdrop underscores that the Dodgers' victory was not just a win but a powerful statement that marked the end of one era of dominance and the beginning of another. The series also unfolded against the backdrop of television's growing importance, with the national broadcasts bringing these iconic moments into more American homes than ever before, expanding baseball's reach and impact.

World Series Game Summaries

The 1963 World Series was a landmark event in baseball history, as it marked the first time the formidable New York Yankees were swept in a four-game World Series. The Los Angeles Dodgers' pitching staff delivered a masterclass in control and effectiveness, allowing just four runs across the entire series. This exceptional performance held the Yankees to an anemic .171 team batting average, which remains their lowest ever in the postseason. Remarkably, the Yankees managed to hold a lead at no point in any of the four games.

Game 1: October 2, 1963, Yankee Stadium (Dodgers 5; Yankees 2)

Sandy Koufax set World Series Record striking out 15 Yankees besting Carl Erskine's record.

Sandy Koufax delivered a legendary performance, pitching a complete game, allowing only 6 hits and 2 earned runs, while striking out a then-World Series record 15 batters. This masterful outing immediately set a dominant tone. The

Dodgers broke the game open in the 2nd inning with 4 runs, highlighted by John Roseboro's crucial three-run home run off Yankees ace Whitey Ford.

The "Left Arm of God" delivers.

Bill "Moose" Skowron singled home Willie Davis in the 3rd inning to extend the lead to 5-0. Tommy Davis also contributed significantly with 3 hits. For the Yankees, Tom Tresh hit a two-run home run in the 8th inning for their only runs, while Whitey Ford took the loss, giving up 5 earned runs in 5 innings. Koufax's record-setting performance delivered a profound psychological blow to the reigning champions, immediately establishing a narrative of Dodger dominance.

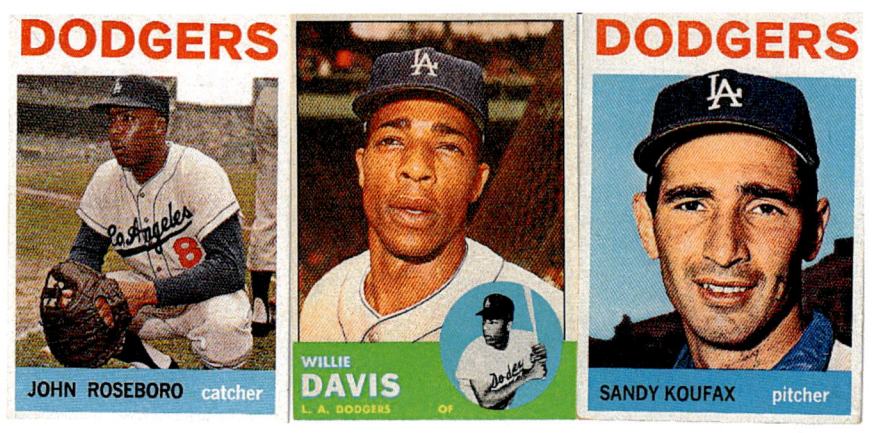

Some of the Stars of Game one from the Author's Dodger Museum Collection.

Game 2: October 3, 1963, Yankee Stadium (Dodgers 4; Yankees 1)

Game two sparked by Willie Davis hit.

Johnny Podres delivered a solid outing, pitching 8.1 strong innings, allowing only 6 hits and 1 earned run, earning the win. Ron Perranoski closed out the game for the save, allowing only one hit in 0.2 innings. The Dodgers' offense continued to produce, with Willie Davis doubling in two runs in the 1st inning. Former Yankee Bill "Moose" Skowron hit a home run in the 4th inning, and Tommy Davis added two triples, including an RBI triple in the 8th.

Game Two starters Al Downing and Johnny Podres.

A significant moment occurred in the 3rd inning when Yankees right fielder Roger Maris left the game after injuring his left arm running into the wire fence that fronts the box seats near the foul pole while chasing Tommy Davis's triple, an injury that forced him to miss the rest of the series. Al Downing took the loss for the Yankees. Podres' strong performance demonstrated the Dodgers' pitching depth, while

Maris's injury was a critical blow to the Yankees' struggling offense.

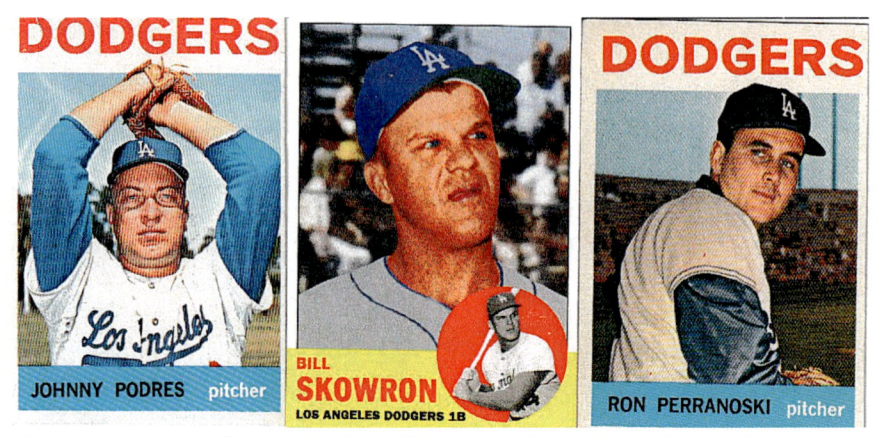

Major Stars of Game Two from Author's Dodger Museum Collection.

Game 3: October 5, 1963, Dodger Stadium (Dodgers 1, Yankees 0)

Don Drydale throws three hit shutout at the Yankees.

Don Drysdale delivered a masterful performance, pitching a complete-game shutout, allowing only 3 hits and 1 walk while striking out 9 batters. Manager Walter Alston later lauded it as "one of the greatest pitched games I ever saw." The Dodgers' lone run came in the bottom of the 1st inning when Jim Gilliam walked, advanced on a wild pitch, and scored on a two-out single by Tommy Davis.

The Yankees could not solve Don Drysdale in Game Three.

Jim Bouton pitched well for the Yankees, allowing only 4 hits and 1 run in 7 innings, but took the loss in a tightly contested pitching duel. The Yankees' offense continued to struggle, managing only 3 hits in the entire game. Drysdale's complete-game shutout provided irrefutable evidence of the Dodgers' unyielding pitching consistency, solidifying the narrative that the Yankees could not generate offense.

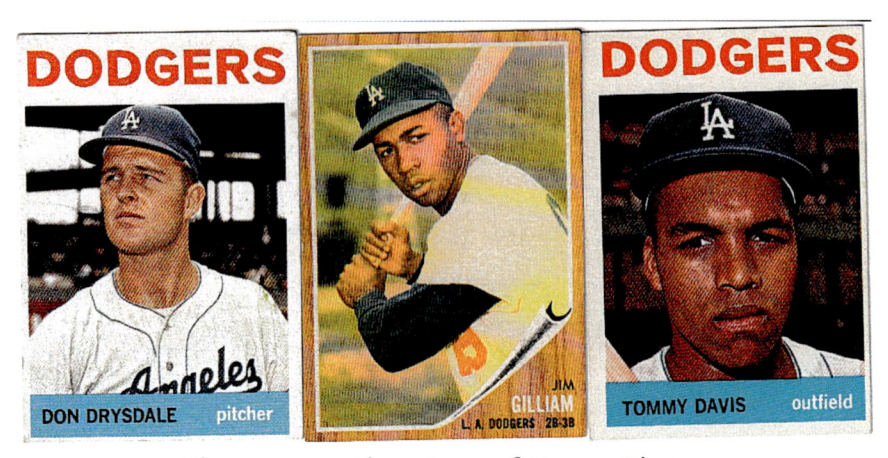

These were the stars of Game Three

Game 4: October 6, 1963, Dodger Stadium (Dodgers 2, Yankees 1)

The Yankees could not solve Koufax either.

Sandy Koufax once again took the mound and delivered another complete game, allowing 6 hits and 1 earned run while striking out 8, earning his second win of the series and the World Series Most Valuable Player award.

Koufax closes out the Yankees.

The Dodgers secured their runs through decisive offensive plays: Frank Howard hit a solo home run off Whitey Ford in the 5th inning to give Los Angeles a 1-0 lead. Willie Davis hit a sacrifice fly in the 7th inning to score Jim Gilliam, securing the winning run. The Yankees' lone run came from a solo home run by Mickey Mantle off Koufax in the 7th inning. Whitey Ford took his second loss of the series. A notable moment during the broadcast saw longtime Yankees announcer Mel Allen's voice give out in the 8th inning, requiring Vin Scully to take over the play-by-play for the remainder of the game – a passing of the torch between two legendary voices of baseball, showcasing Scully's emerging prominence.

Koufax's Game 4 victory provided the definitive statistical culmination of the Dodgers' pitching dominance.

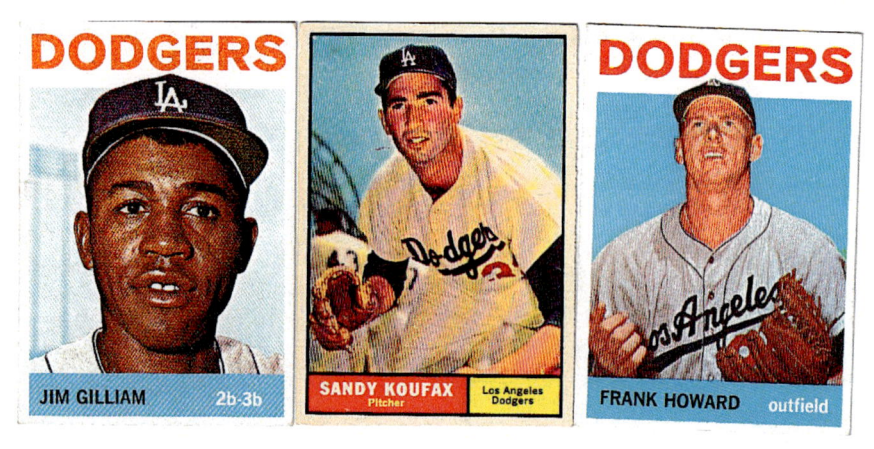

The Stars of Game Four of the World Series.

The Yankees' inability to score more than four runs in the entire series and their lowest team batting average in postseason history (.171) demonstrated a collective, strategic shutdown of a historically potent offense. The sweep, particularly the first time the Yankees had ever been swept in a World Series, was a profound symbolic conclusion to their long-standing dynasty and ushered in a new era of National League prominence.

The 1963 World Series was fundamentally a pitching lesson in baseball, delivered by the Los Angeles Dodgers' formidable quartet of Sandy Koufax, Don Drysdale, Johnny Podres, and ace reliever Ron Perranoski.

It only took four Dodger pitchers to shut down the Yankees in the 1963 World Series

Sandy Koufax's performance was particularly dominant, as he pitched 18.0 innings across two starts (Games 1 and 4), earning both wins. He allowed only 3 earned runs, struck out an impressive 23 batters, and walked just 3. His 15 strikeouts in Game 1 set a new World Series record. Don Drysdale contributed a complete-game shutout in Game 3, pitching 9.0 innings with a 0.00 ERA, allowing only 3 hits and 1 walk while striking out 9. Johnny Podres, in Game 2, pitched 8.1 strong innings with a 1.08 ERA, allowing only 1 earned run and 1 walk, with 4 strikeouts. Ron Perranoski, the Dodgers' ace reliever, played a crucial role, pitching 0.2 innings in Game 2 to earn the save, allowing 1 hit and striking out

1, maintaining a 0.00 ERA in his appearance. The collective effort of the Dodgers' pitchers, combined with their strong defensive play behind them, completely stifled the Yankees' vaunted offense. They held New York to an anemic .171 team batting average, the lowest in Yankees postseason history. Across the four games, the Yankees scored a mere 4 runs.

The Yankees could not solve Koufax either.

1963 World Series Pennant from Author's Dodger Museum Collection.

The Dodgers' pitching dominance in 1963 represents a significant strategic evolution from the previous year. In 1962, manager Walter Alston's bullpen management drew considerable criticism as a trio of relievers combined for over 300 innings, leading to concerns about fatigue and diminished effectiveness. However, in 1963, the overwhelming performance of the starting pitchers—Koufax, Drysdale, and Podres—meant that Alston "did not have to use [the bullpen] as much."

Official 1963 Dodger Team Picture from Author's Dodger Museum Collection.

This suggests a direct cause-and-effect relationship: the lessons learned from the 1962 collapse, particularly regarding bullpen strain, led to a more rested and effective pitching staff in 1963. This strategic adjustment, born directly from the challenges of 1962, contributed significantly to the overall stability and success of the team, demonstrating a direct connection between past adversity and future triumph.

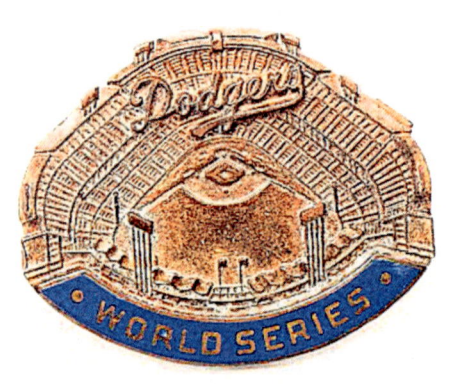

Dodger World Series Press Pin from Author's Dodger Museum Collection.

Walter O'Malley's World Series Ring.

As a final capstone, Walter O'Malley hosted "The President's Championship Dinner" for the Dodgers on October 6, 1963, at The Stadium Club, Dodger Stadium, Los Angeles to celebrate the four-game World Series sweep of the New York Yankees earlier that day. The cover of the dinner menu was illustrated with four aces, a nod to the four straight wins. This 1963 triumph, built on a strong core of players and a refined approach, laid a vital foundation for the Dodgers, many of whom would go on to win another World Series in 1965, solidifying their era of National League dominance.

To crown off the year Sandy Koufax won this 1963 Corvette as Sport Magazine's World Series MVP.

Business and Stadium Development Beyond the game itself.

1963 was a busy year for O'Malley in the financial and operational aspects of the Dodgers:

- **Dodger Stadium Landscaping**: O'Malley, known for his interest in horticulture, invested an additional $1.5 million in 1963 to enhance the landscaping of Dodger Stadium. This effort transformed the ballpark into more than just a sports venue, making it an "oasis and showplace" in Los Angeles with extensive gardens and tree plantings.

- **Tax Dispute**: O'Malley faced a significant challenge on July 23, 1963, when the Los Angeles County Tax Assessor drastically increased the assessed value of Dodger Stadium property to $32.3 million. This would have nearly doubled the team's annual tax bill from $345,000 to approximately $750,000. O'Malley contended the property was worth less, stating he'd "darn right" to sell it for the new assessed value. This began a contentious dispute over the property's valuation. The assessor won.

- **Exploring Dome Technology**: Ever the visionary, O'Malley considered ways to maximize the usage of Dodger Stadium, which he felt was underutilized with only 81 home games per year. In December 1963, he corresponded with renowned architect and inventor R. Buckminster Fuller about the possibility of designing a geodesic dome for Dodger Stadium. The idea was to cover a portion of the field, starting near the infield and extending behind home plate, which would allow for other events like hockey and basketball with covered seating for 20,000.
- **Dodger Stadium Events**: In 1963, several non-baseball events were held for the first time, including Sports Car Road Races in the parking lots; a night of championship boxing matches; filming of an episode of the popular "Mr. Ed" TV show on the field; a public rally for Republican Presidential candidate Barry Goldwater on September 16, 1963 that attracted 42,317 attendees; and just 19 days after the 1963 World Series concluded, a 165-foot ski jump was constructed from the right field side to the left field side of the field as part of the three-day Giant International Ski Show and Grindelwald Ski Swap.
- **Over the Years** Dodger Stadium has seen acts such as The Beatles, Rolling Stones, Fleetwood Mac, Billy Joel, Bruce Springsteen, Elton John, Madonna, Beyonce, Paul McCartney and the Three Tenors, amongst others perform there. Pope John Paul II even held a mass there on September 16th 1987.

Bibliography

Sources Used

Chapter One

D'Antonio, Michael. Forever Blue... Riverhead Books, 2009.
Walter O'Malley Official Website (walteromalley.com).

Caro, Robert A. The Power Broker: Robert Moses and the Fall of New York. Knopf, 1974.

Ballon, Hilary, and Kenneth T. Jackson, editors. Robert Moses and the Modern City: The Transformation of New York. W. W. Norton & Company, 2007.

Jacobs, Jane. The Death and Life of Great American Cities. Random House, 1961.

Flint, Anthony. Wrestling with Moses: How Jane Jacobs Took On New York's Master Builder and Transformed the American City.

Walter O'Malley Official Website (walteromalley.com) - particularly articles like "Wyman's Historic Efforts Bring Dodgers to Los Angeles."

Wyman, Rosalind Wiener (interviews, archival materials, and political records from her time on the City Council would be primary sources, though she did not write a book solely on this topic).

Los Angeles City Council records, historical articles from Los Angeles Times. News/Historical Archives.

Dodgers Stories: 6 Decades in L.A. Documentaries (Wyman appears in this).

Ballparks of Baseball.com (for stadium history and details). Websites/Databases.

Wikipedia articles on Ebbets Field. Websites/Databases.

Brooklyn Public Library archives, historical societies focused on Brooklyn. Local History Books/Archives.

General histories of baseball and the Dodgers that cover the team's time in Brooklyn. Sports Journalism/History Books.

Chapter Two

Associated Press. 1958. "L.A. Dodgers Vote Ahead in Poll." May 24, 1958.

Ballon, Hilary, and Kenneth T. Jackson, eds. Robert Moses and the Modern City: The Transformation of New York. W. W. Norton, 2007.

Ballparks of Baseball.com. n.d. "Wrigley Field (Los Angeles) History." http://www.ballparksofbaseball.com/wrigley-field-la-history.htm.

Baseball Reference. 1958. "Duke Snider Stats 1958." https://www.baseball-reference.com/players/s/snidedu01.shtml.

Caro, Robert. 1974. The Power Broker: Robert Moses and the Fall of New York. Alfred A. Knopf.

D'Antonio, Michael. Forever Blue... Riverhead Books, 2009.

Flint, Anthony. 2007. Wrestling with Moses: How Jane Jacobs Took On New York's Master Builder and Transformed the American City. Random House.

Jacobs, Jane. 1961. The Death and Life of Great American Cities. Random House.

Los Angeles City Council Records. 1958a. "Petition for Referendum on Ordinance No. 110,684." May 1958. Los Angeles City Archives.

Los Angeles City Council Records. 1958b. "Official Election Results, June 3, 1958, Referendum." June 1958. Los Angeles City Archives.

Los Angeles Times. 1957a. "Dodgers Welcomed to L.A. by Throngs." October 24, 1957.

Los Angeles Times. 1957b. "O'Malley Served Summons on Arrival." October 24, 1957.

Los Angeles Times. 1958a. "Dodgers Win First L.A. Game Before Record Crowd." April 19, 1958.

Official MLB Archives. 1957. "National League Correspondence: Concerns Regarding Pasadena Site." December 19, 1957.

Scully, Vin. 2016. Vin Scully: The Voice of the Dodgers. Simon & Schuster.

Sports Business Review. 1959. "Financial Report on Dodgers' Coliseum Tenancy." Vol. 5, no. 3 (Fall 1959).

Sports Journalism Archive. 1960. "Interview with Ed Roebuck." January 15, 1960. [Specify archive/collection].

Walter O'Malley Official Website. n.d. "The History of Dodger Stadium." http://www.walteromalley.com/stadium_history.

Article Los Angeles Times, January 28, 1965

"Dodgers Score Again" Los Angeles Sentinel, December 2, 1971

Peter O'Malley letter to Leonard Koppett May 2, 1978

Chapter Three

D'Antonio, Michael. Forever Blue... Riverhead Books, 2009.

Walter O'Malley Official Website (walteromalley.com).

Caro, Robert A. The Power Broker: Robert Moses and the Fall of New York. Knopf, 1974.

Ballon, Hilary and Kenneth T. Jackson. Robert Moses and the Modern City: The Transformation of New York.

Jacobs, Jane. The Death and Life of Great American Cities (while not solely about Moses, it's a foundational critique of his planning style).

Flint, Anthony. Wrestling with Moses: How Jane Jacobs Took On New York's Master Builder and Transformed the American City.

Walter O'Malley Official Website (walteromalley.com).

Wyman, Rosalind Wiener (interviews, archival materials, and political records from her time on the City Council would be primary sources, though she did not write a book solely on this topic).

Los Angeles City Council records, historical articles from Los Angeles Times. News/Historical Archives.

Dodgers Stories: 6 Decades in L.A. Documentaries (Wyman appears in this).

Ballparks of Baseball.com (for stadium history and details). Websites/Databases.

Wikipedia articles on Ebbets Field. Websites/Databases.

Brooklyn Public Library archives, historical societies focused on Brooklyn. Local History Books/Archives.

General histories of baseball and the Dodgers that cover the team's time in Brooklyn. Sports Journalism/History Books.

Baseball Reference.com. For player statistics and team records.

Robert Shaplen Sports Illustrated "O'Malley and the Angels, March 24, 1958

UPI Story, World Telegram, "O'Malley says Dodgers will stay in L.A." May 26, 1958

Chapter Four

Wills, Maury, with Mike Angeli. On the Run: The Never Dull and Often Shocking Life of Maury Wills. (Autobiography)

D'Antonio, Michael. Forever Blue... Riverhead Books, 2009.

Society for American Baseball Research (SABR). Biography of Maury Wills (often referred to as the SABR BioProject).

Baseball Reference (baseball-reference.com). Player statistics and historical data.

Los Angeles Times, Washington Post, The Sporting News. News/Historical Archives (contemporaneous articles and profiles, which provide primary accounts and analysis from his playing days).

Archival interviews with Maury Wills (including specific mentions of his recollections about the Japan trip and trade, such as from "This Great Game" or similar biographical interviews). Interviews/Documentaries.

Walter O'Malley Official Website (walteromalley.com). Provides context on the Dodgers' move and key events from the owner's perspective.

Chapter Five

Baseball-Reference.com. 1959 Los Angeles Dodgers season.

Baseball-Reference.com. 1959 National League standings.

Baseball-Reference.com. 1959 National League tie-breaker series.

MLB.com Postseason History for 1959. MLB.com.

Baseball Hall of Fame. MLB.com. BaseballHall.org.

Walter O'Malley Official Website. WalterOMalley.com.

Society for American Baseball Research (SABR) Bio Project/Games Project. SABR.org.

Porter, David L. The Dodgers Encyclopedia.

D'Antonio, Michael. Forever Blue: The Story of Walter O'Malley's Dodgers. Riverhead Books, 2009.

Golenbock, Peter. Bums: An Oral History of the Brooklyn Dodgers. G. P. Putnam's Sons, 1984.

D'Antonio, Michael. Forever Blue... Riverhead Books, 2009.

Drysdale, Don, and Bob Verdi. Once a Bum, Always a Dodger. St. Martin's Press, 1990.

Cervenka, Ron. Dodger Stadium: The Official Story of LA's Historic Ballpark.

Los Angeles Times (archival) – Various Staff Writers.

The Sporting News (archival).

Los Angeles Times, August 19, 1978

New York Times August 10, 1978

Chapter Six

Sherry, Larry. Society for American Baseball Research (SABR).

Essegian, Chuck. Society for American Baseball Research (SABR).

Sherry, Norm. Society for American Baseball Research (SABR).

The Los Angeles Times (archival) - Various Staff Writers.

The Chicago Tribune (archival) - Various Staff Writers.

The Sporting News (archival) - Various Staff Writers.

D'Antonio, Michael. Forever Blue: The Story of Walter O'Malley's Dodgers. Riverhead Books, 2009.

Golenbock, Peter. Bums: An Oral History of the Brooklyn Dodgers. G. P. Putnam's Sons, 1984.

Drysdale, Don, and Bob Verdi. Once a Bum, Always a Dodger. St. Martin's Press, 1990.

Chapter Seven

Baseball-Reference.com. 1959 Los Angeles Dodgers season.

Baseball-Reference.com. 1959 National League standings.

Baseball-Reference.com. 1959 National League tie-breaker series.

MLB.com Postseason History for 1959. MLB.com.

Baseball Hall of Fame. BaseballHall.org.

Walter O'Malley Official Website. WalterOMalley.com.

Society for American Baseball Research (SABR) Bio Project/Games Project. SABR.org.

Porter, David L. The Dodgers Encyclopedia.

D'Antonio, Michael. Forever Blue… Riverhead Books, 2009.

Golenbock, Peter. Bums: An Oral History of the Brooklyn Dodgers. G. P. Putnam's Sons, 1984.

Drysdale, Don, and Bob Verdi. Once a Bum, Always a Dodger. St. Martin's Press, 1990.

Cervenka, Ron. Dodger Stadium: The Official Story of LA's Historic Ballpark.

Los Angeles Times (archival) – Various Staff Writers.

The Sporting News (archival).

Chapter Eight

Walter O'Malley Biography. Official Website of Walter O'Malley.

Baseball-Reference.com. 1961 Los Angeles Dodgers Season.

Baseball-Reference.com. 1961 National League Standings.

Baseball-Reference.com. Frank Howard Statistics & History.

Langill, Mark. Dodger Stadium (Images of Baseball). Arcadia Publishing, 2004.

Baseball-Reference.com. Sandy Koufax Statistics & History.

Baseball-Reference.com. Maury Wills Statistics & History.

Baseball-Reference.com. Don Drysdale Statistics & History.

Society for American Baseball Research (SABR). Norm Sherry Biography.

Baseball-Reference.com. Walter Alston Managerial Record.

Official Website of Dodger Stadium. Dodger Stadium History & Construction.

Society for American Baseball Research (SABR). Chavez Ravine and Dodger Stadium: A History.

Jackie Robinson Foundation. Peter O'Malley Biography.

Jackie Robinson Training Complex (MLB.com). Dodgertown History & Integration.

Podair, Jerald. "Haven of Tolerance": Dodgertown and the Integration of Major League Baseball Spring Training.

Walter O'Malley Official Website.

MLB.com. US Civil Rights Trail Honors the Jackie Robinson Training Complex.

The Los Angeles Times (archival) - Various Staff Writers.

The Sporting News (archival) - Various Staff Writers.

Porter, David L. The Dodgers Encyclopedia.

D'Antonio, Michael. Forever Blue... Riverhead Books, 2009.

Pasadena Star-News (archival, for O'Malley's quotes on Angels' rent/parking) - Various Staff Writers.

L.A. Herald & Express (archival, for Autry's quotes on O'Malley's assistance) - Various Staff Writers.

Grabowski, John F. Sandy Koufax. Chelsea House, 1992.

Kahn, Roger. The Boys of Summer (for broader context of Dodgers culture and player perspectives).

Walter O'Malley as told to Joe Hendrickson, Pasadena Star-News, December 31, 1965

Los Angeles Herald & Express, Bud Furillo's Steam Room" April 27, 1961

Chapter Nine

Walter O'Malley Biography. Official Website of Walter O'Malley.

Official Website of Dodger Stadium. Dodger Stadium History & Construction.

Society for American Baseball Research. Chavez Ravine and Dodger Stadium: A History.

California State Supreme Court Records. Fortney v. City of Los Angeles (Case 1959).

Podair, Jerald. City of Dreams: Dodger Stadium and the Birth of Modern Los Angeles. Princeton University Press, 2017.

Henderson, Cary S. "Los Angeles and the Dodger War, 1957-1962." Southern California Quarterly, Fall 1980.

D'Antonio, Michael. Forever Blue... Riverhead Books, 2009.

Porter, David L. The Dodgers Encyclopedia.

Baseball-Reference.com (for general team and player context/dates).

Los Angeles Times. Archival Newspapers.

Los Angeles Examiner. Archival Newspapers.

Los Angeles Mirror News. Archival Newspapers.

Los Angeles Herald & Express. Archival Newspapers.

Pasadena Star-News. Archival Newspapers.

The Sporting News. Archival Newspapers.

U.S. Government Legislative Archives. Federal Housing Act of 1949.

City of Los Angeles Archives. Los Angeles City Council Minutes.

City of Los Angeles Archives. Housing Authority of the City of Los Angeles Records.

City of Los Angeles Archives. Norris Poulson Mayoral Records.

Jackson, Kenneth T., and Hillary Ballon. Robert Moses and the Modern City.

Marsak, Nathan. bunkerhilllosangeles.com, 2024 (Seven-part series about Chavez Ravine).

Los Angeles Examiner May 15, 1959

Sullivan, Neil J. The Dodgers Move West, Oxford University Press, 1987

Los Angeles Mirror News, "The Mailbag", May 6, 1959

Letter to Walter O'Malley from James F, Mulvaney & Ralph Kiner, San Diego Padres, November 5, 1957

Chapter Ten

Fallon, Michael. Dodgerland: Decadent Los Angeles and the 1977–78 Dodgers. University of Nebraska Press, 2016.

Langill, Mark. Dodger Stadium (Images of Baseball). Arcadia Publishing, 2004.

Society for American Baseball Research (SABR) Website (sabr.org).

BaseballReference.com.

BaseballReference.com. For individual player pages: Search for "Frank Howard," "Ron Fairly," "Tommy Davis," "Willie Davis," "Phil Ortega," "Joe Moeller," "Ken McMullen," "Pete Richert," "Dick Calmus," "Sandy Koufax," "Don Drysdale," "John Roseboro." These pages provide birth dates, debut dates, detailed career statistics (including home runs, RBIs, batting average, stolen bases, games played, ERA, wins, losses), rookie status, and team history.

Chapter Eleven

Baseball-Reference.com. This website is a primary source for statistical data, game logs, and player information.

Langill, Mark. Dodger Stadium (Images of Baseball). Arcadia Publishing, 2004.

Newspaper Archives (e.g., Los Angeles Times, San Francisco Chronicle, New York Times): For contemporary accounts of the stadium opening, game recaps, managerial decisions, and fan reactions.

"Dodgers Journal: Year by Year and Day by Day with the Brooklyn and Los Angeles Dodgers Since 1884," published by Clerisy Press (not Arcadia Publishing) in 2009.

Golenbock, Peter. Bums: An Oral History of the Brooklyn Dodger. G.P. Putnam & Sons, 1984.

Wills, Maury, and Mike Celizic. Mighty Maury. Doubleday, 1991. (For direct quotes and personal insights from Maury Wills regarding the 1962 season and Game 1 controversy.)

Snider, Duke, and Bill Libby. Duke Snider's Story: An Autobiography. Simon and Schuster, 1968.

Leahy, Michael. The Last Innocents: The Collision of the Turbulent Sixties and the Los Angeles Dodgers. Harper, an imprint of HarperCollinsPublishers, 2016.

L.A. Dodgers Official Yearbooks/Media Guides (1962-1966). For official team information, statistics, and roster details from the era.

Chapter Twelve

Baseball-Reference.com. For detailed statistics, game logs, and player information for the 1963 regular season and World Series.

Walter O'Malley Website (e.g., WalterOMalley.com). This official site often contains historical documents, photos, and narratives related to Dodger Stadium's development, O'Malley's business interests, and team events like the "President's Championship Dinner."

Newspaper Archives (e.g., Los Angeles Times, New York Times, Sporting News): For contemporary game recaps, journalistic accounts of the World Series, player interviews, reports on the pennant race, and articles detailing Walter O'Malley's business dealings (e.g., the tax dispute, dome exploration).

Langill, Mark. Dodger Stadium (Images of Baseball). Arcadia Publishing, 2004.

Wills, Maury, and Mike Celizic. Mighty Maury. Doubleday, 1991. (For Maury Wills' perspective on the 1963 season, his role on the team, and insights into team dynamics.)

Drysdale, Don, and Bob Verdi. Once a Bum, Always a Dodger. St. Martin's Press, 1990.

Honig, Donald. The Los Angeles Dodgers: The First Quarter Century. St Martin's Press, 1983.

Snider, Duke, and Bill Libby. Duke Snider's Story: An Autobiography. Simon and Schuster, 1968. (While Snider might have been less central in 1963).

"Dodgers Journal: Year by Year and Day by Day with the Brooklyn and Los Angeles Dodgers Since 1884," published by Clerisy Press (not Arcadia Publishing) in 2009.

Buckminster Fuller Institute Archives/Official Website. For correspondence or proposals related to R. Buckminster Fuller's architectural designs, especially concerning geodesic domes and potential collaborations for Dodger Stadium.

Major League Baseball Official Records/Yearbooks (1963).

Production Notes and Compliance Statement

This book and all accompanying materials have been created with full respect for copyright and intellectual property laws.

- All written content is original or properly licensed.
- Historical photographs and memorabilia come from my personally owned collection spanning over 75 years, predating the licensing of agencies such as Getty Images and Alamy.
- Licensed Associated Press (AP) photographs from 1991 and images from trusted sources like Walteromalley.com have been included with proper permission.
- All software tools used—Atticus, Microsoft Word, Grammarly, Affinity Photo 2, Paint Shop Pro, and Textract—were legally purchased and used according to their licenses.
- Research was conducted via reputable sources like Google Search to ensure accuracy. Also included was Newspapers.com

I have complied fully with Kindle Direct Publishing's guidelines and all applicable laws.

Any attempt to dispute the legality of this work without valid evidence will be met with strong legal defense, including action against frivolous claims and abuse of process.

Made in the USA
Monee, IL
17 November 2025

a1fb718f-5f12-4990-a1d6-23d2ee49251fR01